bonding with your bump

The first book on how to begin parenting in pregnancy

DR MIRIAM STOPPARD

London, New York, Munich, Melbourne, Delhi

For Linzi and Will, Beth and

Editor Corinne Roberts
Art Editor Jo Grey
Senior Art Editor Nicola Rodway
Illustrator Anna Hymas
Production Editor Jenny Woodcock
Production Controller Hema Gohil
Creative Technical Support Sonia Charbonnier
Managing Art Editor Marianne Markham
Managing Editors Penny Warren, Esther Ripley
Publisher Peggy Vance

The suggestions in this book are not a substitute for medical advice.
Always consult your doctor or midwife if you have any health concerns.

First published in Great Britain 2008 by
Dorling Kindersley Limited
80 Strand, London WC2R 0RL
A Penguin Company

A CIP catalogue record for this book is available from the British Library

ISBN 978-1-4053-2819-7

Printed and bound in China by Hung Hing Printing Group Ltd

Discover more at
www.dk.com

Contents

Foreword

Many women write to me wanting to be reassured that they'll bond with their newborn baby and looking for answers to questions like:

- Will I feel mother love the instant I hold my baby?
- Is it automatic?
- What if I don't feel a bond straightaway, when will I?
- What if my baby's in an incubator, how shall I bond with her?
- Am I a bad mother if I don't bond straightaway?

The bond of maternal love is mysterious. At least it was. Now we know there's a hormonal orchestra that can switch it on. As labour begins, and for as long as a mother breastfeeds, she has high levels of the most powerful human love hormone, oxytocin, coursing round her body. Oxytocin feeds into the brain's reward centres making us feel secure, calm and well-loved.

Women describe mother love being delayed for 72 hours after the birth. In fact, that's the time when "the milk comes in" and breast milk replaces the nutritious colostrum. Lactation is controlled by another love hormone, prolactin. Together, oxytocin and prolactin can generate powerful mother love and a strong urge to bond with your baby.

What if I don't breastfeed, you may ask, how will I feel mother love and bond with my baby? Don't worry, you will. New mothers have high levels of oxytocin for six weeks after the birth, or even longer, forming a bridge until your bond is well established.

But why wait till after your baby's born to start bonding? You can bond, nurture and start loving your baby from the moment you know you're pregnant. There are many different ways you can do so, through meditation, massaging your bump, talking, singing and having imaginary conversations with your baby.

You can make a very real connection together. You can start to think of your unborn baby as a real person; you may even be able to affect your baby's progress by sending love and encouragement to him. We certainly know that communicating joy to him in the womb can help him to cope mentally in later life.

Your unborn baby is growing not just physically in your womb, she's learning all the time. She's using her developing intellect to remember games you play with her. Your and your partner's voice are imprinted in her brain before she's born. She'll remember songs and music you sing and play while you're carrying her, so bonding with your bump helps your baby's brain to grow healthily.

Research shows you can not only affect your unborn baby's health but you can also affect his health in later life by what you eat during pregnancy.

You can even promote healthy eating habits in your child: your unborn baby "tastes" every food you eat from the fourteenth week of your pregnancy. So if you want an unfussy eater and a child who loves fruit and vegetables, eat them yourself during pregnancy – and again when you're breastfeeding, as these flavours appear in your breast milk.

We also know that visualizing you and your baby having a smooth, easy, joyful birth will help you achieve just that and recover rapidly after the birth. Rehearsing how it will feel to breastfeed your baby makes for a trouble-free start in the early days.

Trusting your body and your baby gives you confidence in your own power and a feeling of control. This in itself helps avert complications during birth and lessens postnatal depression.

Such is the power of bonding with your bump.

benefits
of bonding

As you **talk and play music** to your unborn baby, and massage her through your bump, you can make her feel **calm, tranquil, safe and loved**. When she's feeling this good her brain is bathed in **love hormones** such as serotonin, which help her develop into a **healthy, happy baby**.

During pregnancy, as your baby develops inside you, you may tend to think of her growth only in terms of size, length and weight.

Your unborn child isn't only growing physically but also mentally and psychologically. So much learning and conditioning happen during the nine months you carry your baby in your womb, that its importance cannot be stressed too much. Your influence as your unborn baby's nurturer extends into later life, for the rest of her life.

Scientists see these nine months in the womb as offering your baby a view of the outside world. Cari Corbet-Owen, a South African psychologist, has likened the womb to an amazing classroom for your unborn baby in which she can start experiencing and responding to the world she will be born into. So your bond with your bump is a finely tuned instrument that can start your baby's learning from conception.

One of the most crucial elements in bonding with your baby is your voice. Hearing is one of the first senses to develop and your baby can hear from about 16 weeks from conception. By 27 weeks from conception, all the connections from ear to brain are in place. By six months the womb is buzzing with sounds but your baby can beam in on your voice from all other sounds and with little distortion. To your baby your voice is louder and clearer than it is to people listening to you on the outside. Your baby's heart rate slows because she is interested in the sound of your voice and she sucks faster while you're talking or singing. You are the focal point of her world. It's not just your voice that your baby can distinguish, it's the intonation, phrasing, rise and fall too. It's the

"Your bond with your bump is a finely tuned instrument that can start your baby's learning from conception."

language you speak. In fact after birth, your baby will respond more positively to anyone speaking your language than to any other language, even if she doesn't recognize the voice.

Research involving French and Russian babies revealed how they turned towards the sound of the language they'd been spoken to in the womb. They had become imprinted, literally, with their mother tongue. Some US researchers had mothers read *The Cat in the Hat* repeatedly to their unborn babies. After birth, the babies "chose" the recording of their mother reading the story by sucking at a particular speed that triggered the recording and made it play.

Your mood is likely to affect your baby too. Research would bear out what you'd expect – if you're depressed during pregnancy, your baby will be prone to being unhappy from birth onwards. Furthermore, your baby's unhappiness is in direct proportion to the severity of your depression. Of course your elevated mood keeps your baby happy too and it's natural to experience a mix of moods during pregnancy – it's only if the negative moods outlast the positive ones that they could impact harmfully on your baby in the longer term.

Australian researchers have further shown that babies can remember things that upset their mothers while they were in the womb. When expectant mothers were asked to watch an emotionally upsetting movie clip, researchers observed how babies in the womb were affected. When these infants were exposed to small segments of this same movie clip later, up to three months after birth, they still recalled their earlier response to the movie clip. It seems as if your emotions filter down to your unborn child without your knowing it.

You can see that the future wellbeing of your baby starts at conception. But it's not only your emotional state that will be conveyed to your baby. From about 14 weeks, when your baby's sense of taste is burgeoning, your choice of food can affect your baby's later food preferences. And a healthy diet during pregnancy is one of the key ways in which you can pass on good health to your baby for life.

In one study, three groups of mums-to-be were given a daily glass of either broccoli or carrot juice, while a control group received only water. Later, when their babies had their first solid foods, they ate more cereal if it was mixed with the juice their pregnant mothers had drunk. It makes me wonder if we could avoid those mealtime tussles over eating vegetables if we introduced our children to a wide variety of healthy vegetables while they were still in the womb. And possibly prevent them becoming fussy, faddy or selective eaters – a phase that many children go through. Wouldn't that be a bonus?

In the controversy over alcohol in pregnancy, I wonder if a pregnant woman really understands how what she drinks affects her baby in the womb? For instance when she drinks coffee, even if it's decaf, her baby's breathing and heart rate change, due to all the chemical compounds in coffee. And we also know that just a single measure of vodka in diet ginger ale can stop her baby's breathing movements for up to half an hour within three to 30 minutes of her consuming it, even though her blood-alcohol level is unlikely to be particularly high.

In every way you are the custodian of your baby's healthy development. The more seriously you take your role, the stronger the bond to your unborn baby will be. In a very real sense this bond is vital for the wellbeing of your baby and you can influence your baby's future physical health and her emotional wellbeing by making careful, considerate choices throughout your pregnancy.

It isn't all serious, though, and bonding with your bump can be playful and fun for you both. You can even start playing with your unborn baby by teaching her games through your bump. This is how you do it. Whenever your baby kicks, touch your tummy and say, "Kick, baby, kick!" As soon as she responds, touch a different part of your tummy and repeat: "Kick, baby, kick!" Very soon she'll join in by kicking wherever you invite her to. This is called "spaced repetition" and it's a great way to interact with your little one. Maybe one day, with all this practice, she'll be another David Beckham!

Your unborn baby responds to everything around her, not just to spaced repetition. An event that causes her heartbeat to fluctuate wildly – by up to 30 beats a minute – is sexual intercourse during the last trimester. This cardiac excitement is not, researchers note, harmful to your baby and is directly linked to orgasms experienced by both you and your partner! Your baby feels your excitement in her own womb environment. Astonishingly, an unborn baby needn't have had amniocentesis to be able to detect and respond to a needle entering the womb. Even though their eyelids only open at 26 weeks and most amnios are performed around 20 weeks, babies use some other kind of "vision" to detect the needle and will shrink away from it.

All learning involves memory

Research is providing us with more and more evidence that, even before we're born, we can remember things and have the ability to learn. This is especially so when we repeatedly experience certain words, songs, language, even particular foods. While there may be many factors influencing your unborn baby, I don't think it's too far-fetched to think that a pregnant woman – her life, her moods and her experiences – have the power to mould not just the wellbeing of her baby while in the womb but also her baby's future success and self-belief.

Benefits for you

It's not only your body that alters during pregnancy. Your emotions will fluctuate too and you will experience feelings you've never had before. It's important to recognize that you are bound to feel upset from time to time, that all pregnant women do, and that there are things you can do that will help counteract your mood swings.

Your swinging hormone levels lead to mood changes, from elation to depression. Your changing body shape may temporarily unsettle your self-image. And we're all occasionally beset by fears about our suitability as parents. Emotionally, pregnancy can be quite difficult at times.

Forming an early bond with the baby who is growing inside you can calm your anxieties and emotions. It provides a conduit to channel your feelings which is calming and reassuring. Bonding also makes you start thinking of yourself as a mother, someone who is nurturing, capable and strong, and this builds up your self-belief and self-confidence. You are powerful and capable.

A woman is a very different person from a partner and a partner is a different person from a mother. These changes are profound and sometimes tricky. They involve reinventing yourself in a different form. You have to get used to yourself in a role that's unfamiliar to you. As a woman and a partner you were probably self-confident, capable and independent. Now you may begin to feel apprehensive and possibly even isolated. You're carrying a new life who's completely dependent on you and that may make you feel a temporary loss of identity while you adjust to the idea of becoming a mother.

In fact your bump should make this transition easier. Your bump is evidence that you're stronger than you were, capable of more than you ever thought, fulfilling your natural role as was intended. Your mental state of being pregnant

An insight into yourself

By starting to relate to your unborn baby through keeping a pregnancy diary, for example, you'll begin to get information about yourself that, so far, you haven't recognized and that may surprise or delight you.

Your diary is a place where you can let go of those thoughts and feelings that you may not want to share, and it will also help you to focus on yourself. Your child may also enjoy reading it herself one day – especially when she's about to start her own family.

Taking the time to keep a pregnancy journal means that you will have a cherished record of this special time in your life.

Think of your diary as a conversation with your unborn baby, something that you can read to her when she's older. Better still, read it to your unborn baby so she can start bonding to your voice.

is just as significant a preparation for motherhood as the physical pregnancy, so give yourself time to pause, reflect and talk with your partner about the important and exciting transition into parenthood that you are making together.

A man is different from a partner and a partner is different from a father. Different things are expected of men once they're dads-to-be. Many men will confess to having mixed feelings about the transition to fatherhood. Part of the difficulty is the realization that you're no longer just a couple – you're going to be a family, with all that that implies. For a lot of men, pregnancy is a mystery they feel excluded from. Your bump can be a powerful tool in making your partner

An expression of love

Your baby needs love in the same way as she needs an essential vitamin – more so, in fact. You can't start expressing love too early. As it happens, when you feel love your brain is producing a love hormone – oxytocin – a hormone you continue to have all the way through breastfeeding and that is partly responsible for the mother love you'll feel for your baby whether you breast or bottlefeed. All the hormones your body makes pass across the placenta and they affect your baby too. Oxytocin actually changes the way your baby's brain grows. It helps her brain to develop calming neural connections that quiet fears and anxiety, so that when she gets angry or frustrated she can find ways of soothing herself rather than becoming distressed further.

Bonding with your bump can help to hardwire your baby's brain to respond to discomfort with self-comforting and self-quieting – a very positive skill to encourage, and it's in your hands.

feel included, cementing the new relationships you're all going to be part of. Massaging your bump, talking together to the growing baby inside you, feeling kicks, keeping track of development, going to antenatal classes as a couple – all these activities will bind you strongly together. A man who navigates this transition comfortably is going to be a dad who's supportive and keen to take an active and equal role in being a parent.

While bonding with your bump can put you in touch with your deepest maternal feelings and prepares you for being a mother who finds it easy to express love for her baby in myriad ways, don't be surprised if you have nightmares

"Bonding with your bump can help to hardwire your baby's brain to respond to discomfort with self-comforting and self-quieting."

and strange sleep patterns at the time of conception and around the birth of your baby. Canadian researchers studying 273 women found that the women experienced anxiety dreams about their babies and these dreams were sometimes upsetting enough to make them feel uneasy throughout the day. Investigators at Montreal's Sleep Research Centre found that in 60% of cases new mothers felt compelled to get out of bed and check up on their newborn baby as a result of a dream. The study's author, Tore Neilsen, believes the findings are a window through which to look at emotional bonding in the earliest stages of mother-baby attachment. And sometimes, with love and bonding comes anxiety.

However some women are prevented from expressing love not just for their baby but for themselves. Pregnant women who are physically or mentally abused may find it difficult to relate to their unborn baby and subsequently to their baby after birth. An abusive relationship damages not only a woman's baby and her maternal bond; it also gives her a tendency to suffer from postnatal depression. Even mild abuse can trigger this tendency to PND. Knowing all of this, if you're in a difficult relationship and feel you need help, you should seek to protect yourself, your unborn baby or your newborn baby from the harmful effects of abuse. Talk to your GP or midwife and seek out advice.

In a loving relationship where your partner is involved and supportive, you're protected from PND. In fact your unborn baby "monitors" all your moods. A baby whose mother was prone to depression while she's was carrying a baby will have a similar tendency to depression at birth, in direct relationship to the severity of her mother's depression.

The importance of love
to your unborn baby

The very earliest stages of brain development make all the difference to your baby in her later life. The kind of emotional experiences your baby has with you, starting in the womb, are embedded in her system for life. It's through your brand of parenting when you baby's brain is growing and developing at its fastest that her emotional responses start to take shape.

Stress in infancy, caused by leaving a newborn baby to cry, is particularly painful because, if ignored, it results in high levels of stress hormones that dampen the formation of a healthy brain. Your baby is born expecting to have stress managed for her – by you. Her stress hormone levels will remain low if you – or your partner or another caring adult – keep her content by holding, stroking, feeding, nuzzling, reassuring, whispering and laughing. However, as her emotions are unstable, those stress hormones can shoot up if there's no caring adult alert to her emotional needs and prepared to interact with her as the need arises. To put it as bluntly as Sue Gerhardt in her marvellous book *Why Love Matters*: your baby can't manage her stress hormones, she needs you to manage them for her.

Your baby's system is moulded by how much early stress she has to contend with and how well you help her to deal with it. I believe if you bond with your bump you'll be the kind of mother who helps your baby to recover her equilibrium. If you do, you'll be rewarded with a baby who learns to regulate her own stress hormones and her emotions with them. On the other hand, if she's often left to contend with stress and no one helps her, she'll push out a lot of stress hormones at the least thing. She'll be a baby who cries easily, remains

"The most powerful preventive factor against PND for any woman is the presence of a supportive, sympathetic, hands-on partner, especially in the early days and weeks after the baby is born."

upset despite comforting and is inconsolable. But a baby's vulnerability to stress can start even earlier, in the womb. At this stage, the parts of the brain responsible for handling stress are amongst the most fragile. In pregnancy, an exaggerated stress response may already be starting to form within your developing baby with long-term repercussions.

The healthier, happier and more confident a pregnant woman feels, the less prone she is to stress and postnatal depression (PND). Bonding with your bump can be seen as a preventive against PND. Encouraging your partner to bond with your bump is a further insurance policy. The most powerful preventive factor against PND for any woman is the presence of a supportive, sympathetic, hands-on partner, especially in the early days and weeks after the baby is born. A man who has bonded with his unborn baby is more likely to be that kind of supportive dad and will help make sure your baby blues don't become anything more serious. With that kind of man by your side you're better able to handle stress, lack of sleep, sore nipples, confident in your ability to be a good mother and strong in the choices you'll make for your child. Bonding with your bump helps you both to tap into the resources you never knew you had, as an individual and as a couple, finding inner strength to cope with setbacks and adversity.

Bonding with your bump will shape the mother you'll be

I see bonding with your bump as building a bridge to the kind of loving mother you can be after your baby is born and on throughout your child's life. The kind of mother you are really matters to your baby.

You shape your child for the rest of her life, both to her benefit and detriment. Strengthen your maternal bond from conception and you are already creating the most amazing, exhilarating relationship with your baby.

Nearly 30 years ago, a developmental psychologist, Mary Ainsworth, found that the kind of mother you are shapes and is reflected in your baby's emotional wellbeing later in life. In studying how mothers bonded with and looked after their babies, she found there were three basic mothering styles:
* consistently attentive, responsive and tender
* cold, resentful, rigid
* distracted, erratic in her attention

What she wanted to find out was how the children of these different mothering styles coped with brief separation from their mother a year later. Not surprisingly, she found there were three kinds of reactions:

The first mothering style raised a secure child who saw her mother as a safe haven from which to explore the world and, though upset when she left the room, was reassured when she returned.

The second mothering style led to a child who showed no reaction, either when her mother left or when she returned to the room.

The third mothering style formed a child who was always insecure, holding on to her mother even when they were together, crying loudly when she left the room and remaining inconsolable even when she came back.

A close bond with your baby, formed early in pregnancy and which blossoms and deepens as pregnancy progresses, favours the first kind of mothering style and encourages the emergence of a secure, self-quietening child. This pay-off extends into later childhood and on into adulthood, creating a secure, outgoing individual.

The babies of responsive mothers turn into happy, socially comfortable schoolchildren who are resilient, likeable and empathetic towards others. They have more friends, are relaxed about intimacy, solve problems independently and ask for help readily when they need it.

Children of cold, resentful mothers grow up distant, hostile loners, reluctant to ask for help or comfort, and often with a mean streak, taking pleasure in upsetting other children.

Unpredictable, erratic mothers raise children who are socially awkward, timid, oversensitive, insecure, hungry for attention and easily frustrated.

Make your baby feel
secure and loved

One of the ways you can encourage security in your child is not by rote, routine or rigidly sticking to timetables; it's to react as instinctively to her as you do to your baby during pregnancy.

You'll be a mother who hugs your child when you feel she needs a hug. You'll lift her when you think she wants to be picked up and you'll put her down when she's ready for that. You'll feed her when you think she's hungry and you'll let her sleep when you sense she's tired.

Mary Ainsworth's research showed that every time you act on your natural instincts you're encouraging a happy, secure child. In this way bonding with your bump has tangible, measurable outcomes. It may only seem like gentle massage when you rub and pat your bump but later when you touch and caress your baby in the same way your touch actually activates her growth hormone levels and so you are encouraging robust and healthy development.

Let me explain why feeling secure matters to your baby. In their fine book, *A General Theory of Love*, three American psychiatrists, Professors Lewis, Amini and Lannon, suggest the bond of love, or the lack of it, changes a baby's brain for ever. This is because insecurity in the early days leads to lifelong changes in a baby's brain chemistry. The levels of mood-lifting chemicals like serotonin or dopamine are lowered and blueprinted into a baby's brain in the first few months of life. With the wrong kind of mothering this alteration of brain chemistry becomes hardwired, unchangeable and permanent, leading to timid, clingy children, neurotic, withdrawn teenagers and adults for ever vulnerable to anxiety and depression. In stressful situations, the hardwiring floods the brain with the

"Your baby develops an intuition about love as she divines patterns from her relationship with you. She stores memories of what love feels like."

stress hormone, cortisol, rather than calming serotonin and dopamine. The body and brain are on alert, ready for fight or flight.

To your baby, love means protection. A responsive parent helps a baby to balance her emotions. A baby who's upset depends on her mother to be a reliable source of soothing and comfort because she can't soothe herself. After being soothed many times a baby learns to quieten herself. She knows she's secure, though she's too young to put it into words. She knows implicitly. She comes to know what security feels like.

While in the womb your baby is learning and remembering. We know this because a baby prefers her mother's voice and her native language even when spoken by a stranger within hours of birth. For nine months your baby's brain decodes your voice, your intonations, the rise and fall of your speech and your language patterns. If a baby hears gentle, loving cadences she learns "that love means protection, caretaking, loyalty, sacrifice". If a baby has emotionally unhealthy parents she learns "that love is suffocating, anger is terrifying, that dependence is humiliating" – all crippling concepts that remain for life.

Your baby goes on to develop an intuition about love as she divines patterns from her relationship with you. She stores memories of what love feels like and these eventually make a profound imprint. If you love her unconditionally, if her needs are paramount, mistakes are quickly forgiven, if your patience is endless, and hurts are soothed away, then that is what your child will understand relationships to be and will relate to others in the same way.

Wisdom accumulated
in the womb

While you've been bonding with your bump, your growing baby has been accumulating wisdom and knowledge. How do we know? In her book *How Babies Think*, Professor of Psychology Alison Gopnik and her colleagues describe devising ingenious ways to measure what babies know when they're born and how they think.

Two of the questions scientists ask are: can babies tell two things are the same or different? And if they think they're different, do they prefer one to the other? To answer these questions, scientists have designed a whole new set of technology. They can show babies pairs of carefully controlled items to find out if they can differentiate between them and monitor the babies' preferences.

Using techniques like this it's possible to show that newborn babies can distinguish human faces and voices from the jumble of all other sights and sounds that surround them and that they prefer human faces. Your baby is born knowing she's human. She can only have learned this in the womb.

A few days after being born a baby recognizes and prefers familiar faces, voices and smells to unfamiliar ones. And so a newborn baby will turn to a familiar face, voice or a pad that's been worn next to her mother's skin. Conversely, they'll turn away from other faces, voices and smells.

Babies are even cleverer than that when they're born. Not only can they differentiate between happy, sad and angry faces, they can also fit those faces to the appropriate voices. So if you play a recording of a happy or sad voice, a baby will concentrate on the face showing the emotional expression that matches the emotion they are hearing. She has learned this in the womb, through you.

What babies know from birth

Newborn babies even know how people move. They are so keenly aware of what is human that they're fascinated by an abstract pattern of human movement. As Professor Gopnik explains, her research goes like this:

✳ **You film a person moving in the dark,** the movements only visible through a series of lights on their limbs and joints. Only the moving lights can be seen. Adults can recognize the pattern of lights as distinctly human. So can a baby. She can distinguish that particular human pattern from non-human patterns and, what's more, she prefers it.

✳ **You present babies with two images** – a picture of a human face and a complicated pattern like a chessboard – and record the baby's eye movements. By examining these, you can tell that the baby looks longer at the face, indicating her preference for it.

✳ **You can extend this experiment** by getting babies to suck dummies that are wired up to turn on different videos and audio tapes and find out which ones they choose through their sucking. With this technique, babies will choose to keep their mother's voice playing longer than a stranger's.

✳ **Go one step further** and use the fact that babies get bored easily. Repeat the same pictures and sounds, and babies switch off. Present new pictures and sounds and they become alert again.

✳ **Show a baby a series of smiling faces** and her interest wanes. Show her another happy face, she refuses to perk up. Then show her a sad face and she'll stare hard. She knows all happy faces are the same but that a sad face is different.

Your questions answered

Q How many people can one baby bond with at any one time? My baby spends significant portions of each day with her parents, siblings, extended family, grandparents and regular caregivers? Could she become "overloaded" by being surrounded by a large number of people in this way?

A baby has an infinite capacity to love and an infinite capacity to receive love. There's no limit to the number of people a baby can bond with. This is pretty obvious if you take a look at other cultures. There are many communities on the planet where looking after a newborn baby is not just the job of parents. It's also the job of aunts, uncles, cousins, siblings and grandparents – in fact, the whole community is involved with the upbringing of each child. We know that in this kind of set-up babies do very well.

In fact a baby does best if she's held close to a person's body for most of the first two months of life. In these circumstances, a baby feels secure, well cared for, loved and rarely cries.

Obviously hard-working parents are not always able or may be too tired to carry their child around 24/7 but if couples are surrounded by many willing, loving hands and offers of help, then their burden is shared – to everyone's benefit – not least the baby's.

You should never worry about the number of people your baby comes in to contact with. After all we started out as tribes not families. Secondly, the more love your baby receives, the better equipped for life she'll be. A surfeit of love never did any baby any harm; an absence of love always does.

Q My biological mother gave me up for adoption at birth.
When I first discovered this I felt abandoned despite having
very loving adoptive parents. Will my experience affect the way
I bond with my own newborn baby?

Yes it will, but not in the way that you're worrying about. It will have a very
positive effect. You will bond more closely with your baby, not less. Because
of your experience you will be very aware of moments when you can make
the bond with your baby very strong indeed. And you will instinctively take
advantage of them. Secondly, you have a very strong desire to bond with your
baby and that will make you strive to do so. I would caution you against
expecting too much of yourself. I don't think that bonding with your baby
should be a stick that you use to beat yourself up. I would take things as they
come. All I would suggest is that you look deep inside yourself to find the most
loving parts of you. Get in touch with them and be unafraid of expressing them.
I think you may have forgotten that caring for a baby is an emotional two-way
street. Your baby also bonds to you and the realisation that this is happening
is one of the most uplifting emotions you will ever feel. It results in a virtuous
circle. The tighter your baby bonds to you, the tighter you bond to your baby.

Q Is it possible for me to know the sex of my baby from the shape
of my bump or whether I suffer from morning sickness?

The shape of your tummy is the result of your own body shape and muscle
tone, so is not a reliable indicator of the sex of your baby. Some people say that
if you experience morning sickness you will have a girl. I'm afraid this is also
untrue as morning sickness is caused by low blood sugar and hormones.

Babies are great mimics

The love and security a baby feels in the womb is so important that, astonishingly, newborn babies soon have the talent to see the people who love them more clearly than anything else. So it would seem that babies are equipped with a very deep, innate sense of what it means to be loved and cared for. But babies go further. They'll respond to advances from loving people by imitating them.

Newborn babies prefer faces because they recognize that the face they see is like their own face. They have learned this in the womb. They understand that other people are "like me". Babies are born knowing their deeply personal selves are linked to the bodily movements of other people, movements they can only see not feel. They've learned this in the womb. Babies are born knowing that they are like other people and other people are like them. They learned this in the womb and much more.

Newborn babies are finely tuned to people. The fact is babies flirt – a deeply subtle human interaction. If you hold a tiny baby and start baby-talking to her, within a very short time the baby starts cooing in response to your coos. She smiles in response to your smiles and jerks her body in rhythm with your phrases. Babies even get the timing right. When you talk, your baby listens and stays still. When you stop, your baby seems to know it's her turn and starts vocalizing and jiggling her arms and legs. She's got the gist of conversation and realizes she's connected to you in a special way. That connection doesn't need words, it's a direct human link, and a very sophisticated one at that.

"Babies are born knowing that they are like other people and other people are like them..."

Mirroring facial expressions

Some 30 years ago, Andrew Meltzoff, Professor of Psychology at Washington University and an expert on infant development, showed one-month-old babies imitate facial expressions. That is, if you stick out your tongue the baby sticks out hers. Professor Meltzoff filmed babies being shown someone sticking out their tongue or opening their mouth. He got an independent observer to describe how the baby responded. At the end of the experiment there was a clear relation between what the babies did and what the babies saw.

Professor Meltzoff wasn't satisfied with this. He wanted to show that this talent of babies to imitate was truly innate. So he set up a lab next to the delivery room at his local hospital and arranged for parents to phone him when birth was imminent. For a year he tested babies under a day old, the youngest being 42 minutes old. He found that newborn babies imitated the tongue and mouth movements too.

> **"The fact is babies flirt** – a deeply subtle human interaction... it's a direct human link, and a very sophisticated one at that."

As Professor Meltzoff said, this is truly amazing. A newborn baby has never seen her own face so how could she know whether her tongue is inside or outside of her mouth? She knows. She knows through her consciousness, her internal feeling of her own body. Amazing though it is, newborn babies can only imitate because they appreciate the similarity between that internal feeling, the face they see and the expression it makes.

Why bonding with your
bump is so important

The simple fact is that bonding with your bump will help you to bond, even more closely than you otherwise might, with your newborn baby. If you can establish a relationship with your unborn baby, where you talk to her, sing to her, massage and embrace her through your bump, and share your thoughts and feelings, you're more likely to do these things with your baby once she's born.

I can't begin to tell you what that will mean to your baby in terms of not being fretful, not given to long bouts of inconsolable crying and being able to quieten herself. You'll not just be helping your baby to regulate her emotions with touch, holding, your soothing voice and your breastfeeding but you'll be helping yourself too, by having a contented baby.

Contented babies don't arise from having been left to cry so that they learn they're helpless and powerless to attract your attention. Babies become contented when they learn that their cries for help are heeded and comfort will soon follow, to calm their raging emotions. Sing a song or lullaby to your baby in the womb when you are feeling calm and relaxed and the chances are that the same song will comfort and soothe your newborn baby when she's distressed or anxious.

Let me illustrate just how important loving, caring interest is to babies – and therefore why it's worth cultivating while you're pregnant – by describing what happens to babies in the womb when loving care is absent. Very important work by Professor Vivette Glover of Imperial College, London, on more than 7,000 mums-to-be has shown how stress and anxiety during pregnancy can affect an unborn baby's mental and emotional development. Professor

Theories about stress

Professor Glover's team are working on two theories of how a mother's anxiety can affect the brain development of her unborn baby. One is that anxiety reduces the blood flow to the womb and therefore to the baby, cutting the amount of oxygen and nourishment it receives. The second is that the stress hormone, cortisol, can cross the placenta and affect brain development. To a baby's developing brain cortisol, which in adults is responsible for the fight or flight reflex, is tantamount to a poison. In its presence, helpful brain building hormones like dopamine and serotonin are switched off and brain cells eventually start to die.

But these early experiences of cortisol in the womb may also set up a baby's expectations of what's normal, establishing set patterns which could last throughout childhood. Once these patterns are hardwired in the womb they will control how a baby responds to stressful situations after she is born and possibly for the rest of her life. Reducing anxiety and stress by relaxing and taking gentle exercise is a really effective way of counteracting some of the effects of unavoidable stress.

Glover and her colleague Dr Tom O'Connor researched women in Avon who were expecting their babies between April 1991 and December 1992 in a study named "Children of the 1990s".

Results showed that women who were anxious in the last trimester of pregnancy had children with more behavioural problems. Those who had boys were twice as likely to have a child who showed problems with hyperactivity and inattention (Attention Deficit Hyperactivity Disorder) at age four. The association between anxiety and hyperactivity in girls was less prevalent. It was only those women who scored highest in the anxiety questionnaire who had the increased risk, and these were women suffering from acute stress, not just the normal mood swings experienced by most pregnant women. As I'll go on to discuss in Chapter 3, gentle exercise is a great way to reduce stress levels and your baby will enjoy bathing in the serotonin and endorphins that your body will produce.

So why is reducing stress so important? Professor Glover's study went further, bearing out that a mother's stress levels during pregnancy can have long-term effects on her baby's development. The babies of women who have frequent, bitter rows with partners or who were the victims of domestic abuse scored poorly in mental development tests at 18 months and were slow to talk. The higher the quantity of cortisol in the amniotic fluid, the poorer the baby's mental development. The same babies are also more likely to be anxious and

Relaxing is good for you both

Relaxing to bond with your bump is an antidote to the effects of stress on your baby and it helps lift your mood too.

Taking 15 minutes to chill out, relax, commune with your bump, massage your tummy, whisper to your unborn baby brings down your cortisol levels, and your baby's too.

By **taking time out** to calm yourself, you are also helping your baby's brain to wire itself with calming brain connections and self-soothing hormone pathways – lifelong benefits.

tearful than those born to women who had relaxed pregnancies, so I can't emphasize enough the importance of relaxation and gentle exercise to combat stress and anxiety.

When a mother suffers unpredictable and unavoidable stress her baby also suffers. The nerve cells appear to remember the stress the baby felt in the womb and can fail to grow normally. These deleterious effects on brain development can happen very early in pregnancy, as early as 17 weeks after conception, possibly lowering a baby's IQ. You can see how important it is to counter the effects of stress whenever you can, by deep-breathing and relaxation.

Research continues to reveal much about the development of babies. Professor Katharina Braun, at the University of Magdeburg in Germany, has been studying how a pregnant woman's stress can impede the establishment and maintenance of calming brain connections, particularly in baby boys.

It's clear that a mother's mood directly affects the brain growth of her unborn baby, moulding the behavioural development of her child. It raises the possibility that a programme aimed at reducing anxiety in the most anxious women would greatly help the later behaviour of their children. One of the times when we're most susceptible to the influences that surround us is when we're developing as an unborn baby. So try to remain as free as possible of negative stress during pregnancy. Don't be afraid to ask for support and reassurance from family, friends and employers so that you can have a happy and healthy pregnancy. And don't be afraid to lean on people who want to help.

Bonding with your bump and creating a harmonious environment in the womb goes a long way to creating a relaxed newborn baby and also starts you off early on your own lessons in parenting, developing the nurturing skills that will help you to raise a happy child. Bonding with your bump equips you to be a loving, tuned-in parent.

Your body, your baby

It's not really surprising that your unborn baby is so sensitive to your state of mind and body, since your body is temporarily the home of your baby. You share everything, the good things and the not so good, so even your stress levels become hers.

This means that during pregnancy you can pass on your own oversensitized stress response to your baby – and your baby becomes "supersensitive" as a result. Mothers who drink a lot of alcohol in pregnancy can raise the stress hormone level in their unborn babies, and there's some evidence that these children will be supersensitive, and have an overreactive stress response that lasts into adulthood. Smoking during pregnancy not only affects growth but has also been found to affect a baby's behaviour, making her moods swing between fussiness and indifference.

Babies exposed to stress-inducing experiences in the womb are more likely to appear to be "difficult", supersensitive, from the start. Supersensitive babies are more easily stressed. They react more intensely than other babies to noise, light, temperature fluctuations, hunger, thirst. They're not simply more demanding, they also need a lot of love and care to keep them on an even keel and the balance can be a tricky one to maintain.

Parents of supersensitive babies have to work harder at soothing and calming, holding and feeding often so that their babies gradually learn to be less sensitive. Parenting styles can go a long way to making sensitive babies more secure. A Dutch researcher, Dymphna van den Boom, wanted to find out if mothers could learn to manage their babies in a way which calmed their supersensitivity. She drew up a programme for mothers of sensitive babies which aimed to help the mothers to respond differently to their babies. With this help, most of these more sensitive, "difficult" babies grew up secure and happy.

"Just the **physical act of smiling** releases feel-good hormones into your bloodstream. These hormones cross the placenta **so your baby can enjoy them too** and is soothed and calmed."

Your smile is so important to your newborn baby that I'd suggest that you to start smiling at your bump in readiness to interact with her in those first days and weeks after her birth. Just the physical act of smiling releases feel-good hormones such as serotonin into your bloodstream. These hormones cross the placenta so your baby can enjoy them too and is soothed and calmed. Well-loved babies come to expect you to respond to their emotions and feelings so that they calm down. Through you doing it for her, your baby eventually learns how to do it for herself.

This early loving relationship with you has a great impact on your baby because she's so unformed and delicate. Without the right conditions to develop, certain biochemical systems can become set in an unhelpful way. The hormones that control emotions can be adversely affected. Even the brain, growing at its most rapid rate in the first year and a half, may not develop properly.

So how does your baby become a social being? To a newborn baby feelings are very basic – distress or contentment, discomfort or comfort. Slowly your baby starts to recognize pleasant things; the soothing image of you coming through the door smiling when she cries in her cot. She begins to store them as images.

When your baby pays close attention to you, the emotions she sees in your face and gestures communicate with her brain; when your baby sees you are happy, this vision of you activates her brain to feel happy too. She resonates with your feelings. And in helping your baby resonate with positive feelings, you help her social brain to grow. This is what I mean when I say your baby's relationship with you is the blueprint for all other relationships.

This social part of the brain is called the orbitofrontal cortex and it's virtually non-existent at birth. Without a loving relationship with you, your partner or other caring adult your baby's orbitofrontal cortex may not develop well.

There's a critical window of opportunity in growing this social part of the brain. If your baby doesn't have a loving relationship with you during the period in which this part of the brain normally develops (up to the age of three years), there's little hope of fully recovering that lost friendliness or of developing this part of the brain adequately, hard though this fact may be for us to accept.

Your baby can't develop an orbitofrontal cortex on her own. She depends on a good relationship with you, your partner, or other loving adult for this to happen. You can get your baby hooked on good times with you by making them highly pleasurable. If the relationship with you is pleasurable, you and your baby are unconsciously developing her ability to be self-quieting and promoting the healthy development of the social part of her brain, the orbitofrontal cortex.

Your baby's first pleasures are warmth, security and the sound of your voice in the womb. Touch is powerful too because your baby was held firmly in your womb. Being lovingly held is the greatest spur to growth, more so even than

"Lots of good experiences early on in life produce brains with more neural connections... with more connections there is better brain performance..."

The chemistry of your smile

Another researcher, Allan Schore, believes your looks and smiles actually help your baby's brain to grow. Schore suggests that it's positive looks which are the most vital stimulus to the growth of the social, emotionally intelligent, brain.

When your baby looks into your eyes and sees happiness, her own brain becomes pleasurably aroused and her heart rate goes up. Both these things trigger a chemical cascade of happiness. First, a pleasure hormone called beta-endorphin is released into the circulation and specifically into the orbitofrontal region of the brain. These natural opioids help brain cells to grow by controlling glucose and insulin. They also make your baby feel good. At the same time another hormone called dopamine is released from the prefrontal cortex. This too enhances the use of glucose helping new brain cells to grow. This energizing and stimulating effect is part of what we feel when we anticipate reward. All those doting looks fire off the pleasure chemicals that actually help the social brain to grow.

breastfeeding. Held by a smiling parent your baby is safe and warm, muscles relax and breathing deepens as tensions fade through gentle stroking and rocking. Your baby's heart will synchronize with yours. If you're relaxed and calm, your baby will be too. Your baby's chemical responses to you also promote the activation of genes to promote healthy development.

All this depends on the number of good experiences your baby has. Lots of good experiences early on produce brains with more neural connections – more richly networked brains. With more connections there is better brain performance and a more flexible ability to use particular areas of the brain. In the tender care of your smiles and loving looks, between 6 and 12 months, there's a massive growth spurt of these connections in your baby's brain at just the time when the pleasurable relationship with your baby is most intense. The bonds between you get really strong.

The very helplessness of babies encourages this unbreakable bond between you. In turn this generates the chemicals that promote brain connections and brain growth which will never be as rapid again. The more you smile, the more you're helping your baby's brain to grow.

By the same token a newborn baby remembers and stores negative looks and incidents. A negative look can trigger a chemical response, just as your positive look can. Your disapproving face can set off stress hormones which stops the flow of endorphins and dopamine and also kills the pleasurable feelings they bring.

Using PET (Positron Emission Tomography) scans, scientists have shown that a strong maternal relationship actually changes the way a baby's brain develops. The pre-frontal lobes are brought to life and programmed by a strong mother-baby bond. In the mid 1980s, an American sociologist, Dr David Olds, studied 400 mothers in the state of Minnesota. Half were given intensive support from health visitors to help them bond with their babies in the early days and weeks after birth and half were not. Fifteen years later, when he followed up on his research, he discovered that the children of mothers who'd been helped and supported by health visitors to form a strong maternal bond were 50% less likely to have been arrested.

From 10–18 months, the human brain develops a talent for storing images and the emotions that go with those images. Negative images can become etched in the memory. The

"The more you smile, the more you're helping your baby's brain to grow."

stored images also become an important tool of emotional control for your baby. In future situations with similar types of emotional arousal, a toddler will use them as a guide to behaviour in your absence. But without your lessons in soothing and calming your baby remains vulnerable to stress, which can quite often escalate into overwhelming distress.

Most newborn babies are ready to bond immediately after birth – indeed, it is a survival strategy on your baby's part, as without you she won't thrive, she's entirely dependent on you for everything. However, it may take you a little longer to bond, to feel the outpouring of love that will sustain you through the inevitable sleepless nights and all other rites of parental passage. Bonding can be instant, a rush of overwhelming love from the moment you set eyes on each other, or it can take time. Classical mother love usually kicks in 72 hours after the birth, when your breasts make milk under the influence of oxytocin, the "love hormone" which is present in women's bodies for six to eight weeks after giving birth.

Building a support network is vital to bonding. It's important that you and your partner have people around you who can help you through the transition into parenthood. If during pregnancy the two of you build on your teamwork together, then the transtion to parenthood will be smoother. In the first few days and weeks of being parents, don't be afraid to lean on the friends, family members and neighbours who offer their help. And don't underestimate how important a stable home environment will be, over the years, to your child. Children from stable, loving homes are physically healthier, do better at school and are happier human beings than children from homes that are fragmented or chaotic. And it all begins here, in the nine months of pregnancy and those first few precious days following the birth of your child.

Your questions answered

Q Does every parent fall instantly in love with their newborn baby? Is bonding instinctive and which hormones are responsible for it?

It is – as instinctive as hormones are. In the first days and weeks after birth our maternal instincts are hormone-driven. We actually have a hormone for mother love: it's called oxytocin and it is one of the hormones involved in lactation and the production of breast milk. Lactation proper starts about 72 hours after delivery. Before then, your baby is nourished with the rich, clear, straw-coloured liquid in your breasts called colostrum.

In the waiting period for breast milk it's quite common for women to wonder where their maternal instincts are. It's not unusual to feel very little for your baby. But as soon as the milk "comes in" under the irresistible force of oxytocin and a second hormone called prolactin, mother love usually assaults us with a force that can be surprising, and we have no way of resisting it. Sometimes it completely overwhelms us. This is because these lactation hormones affect the reward system in the brain which make us feel both loving and well loved. The feeling is very addictive and is one of the reasons why women, once started on breastfeeding, don't want to give it up.

Mother love, of course, arrives after birth even if you decide not to breastfeed because women are producing small amounts of oxytocin all the time. You just won't have the full-on flood of it which is part and parcel of breastfeeding. Then, once the hormones have got you going, your maternal bonding makes sure your mother love is here to stay.

Q I'm adopting a newborn baby girl. How can I best bond with her?

I honestly think you should read some accounts of how women feel about their adopted babies. I have a niece who recently adopted a baby boy. He wasn't the newborn baby who's very easy to bond with. By the time she got him he was very nearly 16 months but this baby was so longed for, so treasured, so cherished that in all honesty he has become the love of my niece's life and she's very open about expressing her feelings. Why don't you get in touch with the BAAF (British Association for Adoption and Fostering – www.baaf.org.uk) who will have links to brochures containing accounts of couples' love for their adopted baby and you'll realize instantly what an amazing experience is in store for you. Keep thinking to yourself what a gift your little girl is going to be. In a way you could love her more than your own child because finding her has been such a journey, sometimes problematical. You had to try harder and longer to fulfil your strong desire to have a child. Think of how she is the fulfilment of your yearning and therefore a cause for huge celebration. If you bear all these thoughts in mind you can make every moment spent with your adopted baby a celebration. Show her in every way you can the blissful happiness she brings to your life and you'll be astonished by how strong your bond turns out to be.

Q When will I first feel my baby move in my tummy?

You will probably experience a feeling not unlike wind, a brief fluttering sensation, in your tummy at around 20 weeks of pregnancy. It's a thrilling feeling and will help both you and your partner bond strongly with your unborn baby whose presence you can now, quite literally, feel.

CHAPTER 2

becoming
parents

As your pregnancy progresses, so you and your partner have time to **adjust to the idea** of becoming parents. Along the way you will **probably feel exhilaration, excitement** and some moments of anxiety as you travel through uncharted waters **together into parenthood.**

The first trimester

No matter how much you both may have planned your baby and how much you want him, you'll be ambushed by your emotions on hearing the news that you're expecting. Having a baby means that life will never be the same again. Life will be different in so many ways but, rest assured, once you make the transition from couple to family, it will eventually be rewarding, fulfilling and satisfying.

However, few people feel that at the beginning. In fact you may feel the opposite – in equal parts with the joy, elation and excitement. Your fears and anxieties are partly because you're expected to spin on a sixpence – suddenly you're going to be a mum and a dad and there's a great deal to take on all at once.

Men and women respond differently to the news of pregnancy; elation may fade into fear, anxiety or depression at the thought of the responsibilities looming, and the changes that are unavoidable. Changes in relationships can be unsettling and tricky to deal with at the best of times. Changes that take place in early pregnancy are particularly taxing because they have to be played out when you're feeling tired and possibly anxious, and both you and your partner may be feeling ambivalent about your new situation. Use the months ahead to prepare, as much as possible, for what's in store, and really enjoy your pregnancy. If you can, go away for a weekend or have a holiday when you're between four and seven months pregnant and it will give you both plenty of time and space to share your feelings together. In the years ahead you'll probably look back on it as the end of your old way of life, in the run up to the exciting new times ahead.

Emotionally, pregnancy can be a roller coaster. Enormous changes occur in your body during pregnancy and, because of this, your mood is likely to swing frequently. It's not unusual to find yourself becoming hypercritical and irritable, your reactions to minor events exaggerated. Sometimes you'll feel unsure of yourself and panicky, and you may even have bouts of depression and crying, followed by periods of elation.

It's normal to feel all of these things, because you're less in control of your feelings than usual. Powerful pregnancy hormones are kicking in and influencing your moods the way a conductor leads an orchestra. So there's no reason to feel guilty or ashamed if you show irritation, anger, or frustration. If you explain the situation, most people will be understanding.

All sorts of conflicting feelings

Even with the most positive frame of mind as you go through pregnancy it's normal to have conflicting feelings from time to time. One moment you're thrilled at the prospect of starting a family, the next minute you're a little daunted by your new responsibilities, wondering how you will make all the adjustments that being a parent demands.

You and your partner will start to come to terms with the pregnancy and begin to think about what it really means. Until now your thoughts about a baby and parenthood may well have all been in soft focus, a rosy but distant picture of a loving threesome. Now it's for real.

Conflicting feelings are sure to surface once you begin to adjust to your new situation. It's normal and you shouldn't worry about it. It means that you're genuinely accepting the changes and will be prepared to face all eventualities.

It's normal to have fears and most women worry about labour – whether they'll be able to cope with the pain, whether they'll scream or defecate, or need an episiotomy or emergency Caesarean, but there's really little need to be anxious about any of these things. Labour is usually straightforward and how you behave during labour is of little or no importance. You may be surprised at how calm you are; you may not be calm at all, and that's okay too. Just remember that your

Will my baby be affected by my mood?

You may worry that your moodiness will affect your baby. Although your baby does react to your moods, like kicking when you're angry or upset, changing emotions appear to have no detrimental effect as long as there's a balance between the good moods and the bad.

Dreams and nightmares can be very vivid, and you may find that you wake up abruptly – hot, drenched in sweat, and with your heart racing, but this won't harm your baby, either.

The upside is your baby really enjoys your good moods – your excitement, your happiness, and your elation. When you feel good, your baby feels good. When you're relaxed, your baby is also feeling tranquil.

If some activity makes you content and happy – listening to music, dancing gently, painting – do as much of it as you can and share the feeling with your baby.

birth attendants have seen it all before, are there for you, so there's nothing for you to feel embarrassed about. It's legitimate to worry about how good a parent you'll be, whether you will hurt or harm your baby, or not care for him properly. If you don't know much about baby care and are worried about doing a good job, get some hands-on experience. Handle and care for a newborn baby if you can. Perhaps you could babysit for a friend's baby, or spend some time with him. If you change and feed her baby you will probably gain confidence, especially if you encourage your partner to change and feed him too. Try to get fears into perspective – you probably had similar worries about starting a job and you made out all right. Joining an antenatal class, looking at pregnancy books, magazines and websites – all these will help give you the information you and your partner need about pregnancy and will help you both feel involved and informed every step of the way. The more informed you are, the more confident you will be.

You may find you're dreaming more often and your dreams may sometimes be particularly vivid and frightening, especially in the last trimester. Your dreams express deep feelings and concerns that are entirely natural – everybody worries at one time or another that something will be wrong or go wrong with their baby. You may have dreams about losing the baby and this is usually an expression of fear about miscarrying or having a stillborn baby.

Dreams like these protect you because they prepare you for a sad outcome and they're also a way of bringing these feelings to the surface. In a way, they act as a release for your anxieties. Don't make the mistake of taking dreams literally and then feeling guilty or frightened. Talk your dreams over with your partner.

"Joining an antenatal class, looking at pregnancy books and magazines – all these will help give you the information you need about pregnancy."

"Your dreams can be seen as a kind of rehearsal for what you expect to happen when your baby is born and to accustom you to what lies ahead."

We sleep to dream and rest. Dreaming is the brain's way of clearing out the circuits, recharging the batteries and starting afresh. Dreams often reflect our psychological state, though not always in an obvious way. They naturally reflect your mental state when you're pregnant and this mental preparation is just as important a preparation for motherhood as the more physical aspects of pregnancy and birth.

In the first trimester your dreams are often separated from the fact that you're pregnant, probably as a way of protecting you in case the pregnancy ends prematurely. So your dreams tend to be about the past.

As your pregnancy progresses and you safely enter the second trimester you can feel free to start thinking of your baby as a real person and bond very tightly with him. You then start to have anxieties about the final outcome of your pregnancy. Will the baby be OK? Will you manage labour? Will you turn out to be a good mother? Will your baby be healthy and thrive? Will something unpleasant happen to your baby? These themes are reflected in your dreams, not necessarily exactly but through metaphors for anxiety – missing planes and trains, not being able to get to an exam on time, finding yourself on a stage and you can't remember your lines.

In the third trimester you may dream even more vividly that the baby is born abnormal, deformed or very small. And you may find natural phenomena figure in your dreams – volcanic eruptions, whirlwinds, the sea, storms, dams and water. So your dreams can be seen as a kind of rehearsal and mental preparation for what you fear may happen when your baby is born and to accustom you mentally and prepare you for what lies ahead.

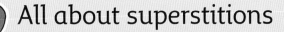

All about superstitions

Nearly every pregnant woman becomes more superstitious than normal. Superstitions and old wives' tales were, in the past, ways of attempting to explain an inexplicable world and make sense of apparently random events that occurred in it.

With the excellent medical care now available, your chances of having a damaged child are very low, and what you might interpret as a bad omen, bringing bad luck, certainly doesn't mean that anything will go wrong with your baby.

For women, the first pregnancy is uncharted territory but for men, once removed as they are from the physical experience of pregnancy, it can sometimes be truly confounding.

Many men start off from a position of pretty terrified ignorance and try to make up by forcefeeding themselves with information. It's difficult to make sense of because a man has no idea what being pregnant is actually like. The confusion is compounded unless men can be encouraged to discuss their feelings about parenthood. In the nine months leading up to the great day, women seem to talk of nothing else while some men want to talk about anything but!

A survey of more than 2,100 Brits found that, despite wanting to be good dads, today's father is retreating into the rather authoritarian manner of his own father. These men were "new men" until they became new fathers, which is why they're so disappointed when they fail to be the sort of dads they wanted to be. Despite pictures of male icons with young babies, such as the footballer David Beckham and the Coldplay singer Chris Martin, society offers few role models for fathers.

One in five feels that he's a worse parent than his own dad and not up to the double duty of work and home. The disappointment and sense of failure can make men shut down emotionally and admit to being depressed and pessimistic about their parenting skills. Many fathers want to simplify their lives after having children and to do that they may end up trying to escape the demands of family life by spending longer hours at work, especially if financial pressures are greater than now than they were before.

Sadly this can be reflected in fathering styles – some dads tending to avoid emotional involvement with their children, a quarter not talking about personal issues with their children and one in five becoming less involved in their children's lives than their own parents were.

Many dads try to bond with their children through schoolwork but scarily half of all dads agree with spanking, compared to just over a third of mothers, something which is likely to alienate children from their fathers even more.

With his son Matthew, Professor Laurie Taylor wrote the book *What Are Children For?*. He believes that the status of fatherhood has been undermined by modern life which has left fathers with nothing for their children to inherit. There's nothing obvious for a father to do or to be. The world is changing rapidly and children may spend increasing amounts of time isolated in their own rooms, on the internet or playing computer games.

Matthew Taylor disagrees with his father. He believes modern fathers can do more for their children than dads of any previous generation. As men stay younger in their lifestyle for longer, the chance to become mates with their sons has

"Your growing bump can be a powerful tool in making your partner feel included, cementing the new relationships you're going to share."

How to make dads feel welcome

In his great book *Is There a Father in the House?*, James Torr makes suggestions which put a welcome and healthy male point of view:

✻ **Make sure there's a chair for your partner** to sit on in antenatal clinics and scan rooms, so the two of you feel equally welcome and at home.

✻ **Be careful not to overemphasize his supporter role.** Dads want to help their partners, but also want recognition as parents.

> "A man who navigates this transition will be a dad who's supportive and wants an equal role."

✻ **It's helpful if you talk everything through** before the baby arrives. Listen to his feelings and perhaps agree on sleeping arrangements, including which time of night you each most need valuable sleep.

✻ **Chat to him about attending the birth** so he can begin to explore his feelings and expectations of parenthood.

✻ **If possible make sure books,** leaflets and information for parents are given to you jointly rather than just to you.

✻ **Remember that if he appears to be** "hanging back" this does not necessarily mean he doesn't want to engage with the baby. It could be that he expects all questions and remarks to be addressed to you.

✻ **Don't assume that a fathers' group** is the best place for an expectant father. He may identify with "parenthood" and be more comfortable among mums and dads.

increased. Research shows, for example, that dads who read books and newspapers regularly at home are a positive reading influence on their children. Children have their teenage crises earlier now, so they relate to their fathers as adults earlier. And the tendency for children to stay at home until much older has meant they have longer to bond with their dads – all good opportunities, if dads will take advantage of them, to be a positive role model for their children.

Being an involved dad

In one of your bonding sessions say, when your partner is massaging your bump, read this through together to reconfirm your commitment to being parents, sharing your hopes and expectations with each other.

✻ **It's your baby too**. We're in this together. I couldn't do it without you.

✻ **Talk with me about your feelings.** Express your concerns openly and freely, so I can see things from your point of view.

✻ **Let's write our own ideal birth plan** so we can share all our arrangements and plans for the birth and meet any professionals involved beforehand. Let's visit the hospital and delivery room together, so we know our way around.

✻ **Come to antenatal classes with me** so that you can hear your baby's heartbeat and see him on the ultrasound monitor.

✻ **Be present at the birth as my birth partner** so we can share those precious moments together. I need you there with me, to support and encourage me.

Ask your partner what kind of dad he'll be

New dad …

✳ You have an affectionate time with your child, when you can both relax and let the relationship evolve naturally.

✳ You comfortably discuss emotions and sexual issues.

✳ You feel comfortable in your role as father, and not as though your partner is the primary parent.

✳ You prioritize the needs of your child over your work responsibilities, getting up in the night and leaving work early if need be.

✳ You regularly put your child to bed, take him to nursery, read to him and look after him without the mother present.

Arm's-length dad …

✳ The time you spend with your child is largely "project-based", helping with schoolwork assignments, for example.

✳ Your chats with your children revolve entirely around structured activities and avoid emotional discussions.

✳ You feel your partner is the real expert in parenting and that you depend on her guidance, rather than taking the initiative yourself.

✳ You prolong your day at the office to reduce the time you spend at home and would never consider prioritizing home over work.

✳ You feel that other men's apparent ease with fatherhood outstrips yours so much that your most valuable contribution is as the breadwinner.

"Massaging your bump, talking together to the growing baby inside you, feeling kicks, keeping track of development, going to antenatal classes together – all this binds you as a couple."

The second trimester

While you're sailing into calmer waters – your baby is growing, your sickness has gone, you have incredible energy – your partner could still be confounded by what's happening. A study of men whose partners were expecting has shown that the vast majority experience "pregnancy symptoms", ranging from food cravings to swollen stomachs. The men were so attuned to their partners that they started to get the same symptoms.

When a group of 282 expectant fathers aged between 19 and 55 were monitored through each stage of the pregnancy and the results compared to a control group of 281. In the study, the majority of men developed symptoms including mood swings, morning sickness and even pseudocyesis – where the abdomen swells to mimic a pregnant stomach. So expectant fathers can have sympathetic pregnancies too!

With the exception of the false "baby bump" which continued to grow post-partum, symptoms gradually worsened throughout the early stage of pregnancy, peaked during the third trimester and disappeared shortly after birth.

Stomach cramps were among the most common symptoms. One father-to-be said he felt as if he was giving birth. "My stomach pains were very much like a build-up of a woman's contraction as she's giving birth. They started mild and then got stronger and stronger and stronger," he told researchers.

Closely following were morning sickness and changes in appetite. One dad admitted: "I had an unstoppable craving for chicken kormas and poppadoms. Even in the early hours of the morning."

No one knows the exact reason why men experience sympathetic symptoms,

"Once your partner sees your body has begun to change and, later, **when he feels the baby move, the idea of having a baby** becomes more real."

also known as Couvade Syndrome, but men are not simply trying to "muscle in". His sympathetic pregnancy could be the expression of how much he is looking forward to being the dad you hope he'll be.

Far from being attention-seeking, these symptoms are entirely involuntary. Often the men haven't got a clue about what's happening to them. Doctors don't recognize Couvade Syndrome – there's no medical diagnosis – yet this research proves that Couvade Syndrome really exists. The results of this study, the largest of its kind ever carried out in the UK, were echoed by the experience of midwives who have noticed that men often complain of nausea during the early stages of their partner's pregnancy.

Your pregnancy may not have seemed real to him for the first few months, not least because physically you looked the same as you did before becoming pregnant. But your partner's probably worrying that he feels differently from you about the pregnancy; it's an internal experience for you and an exciting but external one for him, and the two of you don't suddenly become one person with one set of thoughts, feelings and reactions just because you're now having a baby together.

However, once your partner sees that your body has begun to change and, later, when he feels the baby move, the idea of having a baby becomes more real to him. It's at this time that his feelings of excitement may be tinged by concerns and niggling worries; whatever your family set-up, it's normal for him to begin to worry about being able to provide for his family. Having a child can be an extra financial burden, especially if you're going to give up your job, but try not to make

life-changing decisions, such as his getting a new job or seeking promotion. It's difficult to know whether he'll want extra responsibility at work a year down the line, once he's a parent. Remember, as a father, he has much more than just material possessions to offer your child.

It's never too soon to start practising so if your partner really wants to get to grips with what it feels like to be pregnant you could read this next bit together, if only for a laugh. Baby Matters, a Manchester-based project aimed at reducing teenage pregnancy, is trying out a new product – the Empathy Belly Pregnancy Simulator – on young people so they can get a better understanding of pregnancy, but any expectant father could try it, to see how it feels to be pregnant. The Empathy Belly mimics for the wearer the changes to a body's centre of gravity during pregnancy – including foetal kicking, shortness of breath, flushing sensations, bladder pressure and the fatigue induced by carrying extra weight. Expectant fathers can wear the Empathy Belly and greatly increase their sense of involvement, instinctive awareness and empathy for their partners. Realizing firsthand that the discomforts are genuine and that pregnancy requires significant effort and adjustment on a woman's part, expectant fathers feel a surge of appreciation for their pregnant partner and begin to communicate more openly and to be more supportive and understanding.

The Empathy Belly is filled with warm water. Then you have a sandbag that sticks to the underneath of your tummy so that it feels as if the baby is pressing on your bladder. There are two lead balls that function as the limbs of the baby and there are also built-in breasts. It gives girls the idea of just how big they'll get

"You'll probably seek out other expectant parents to **share your excitement** and check out your anxieties. **It's reassuring to swap notes.**"

and boys begin to understand what it's like to be pregnant. Good for any expectant dad. The project also uses virtual babies: teenagers take the babies home for the weekend, during which time the babies are programmed to need a great deal of care – a valuable rehearsal for when the baby arrives for any dad-to-be.

Sometimes expectant parents don't bargain for the fact that their relationship with family and friends will change. For a start you'll probably seek out other expectant parents to share your excitement and check out your anxieties. It's reassuring to swap notes. It's also thrilling to see how pleased everyone is for you. It probably feels like a graduation and in many ways it is. You're graduating to parenthood. You'll probably find that some relationships will strengthen – with your parents and grandparents – and you'll form new ones with friends and neighbours who have recently become parents.

If you want to hang on to your child-free friends or those who have older children, look at their relationships with other couples who have recently become new parents. Keep a weather eye out for the vacant, glazed look that lets you know they find a baby's wicked way with rusks less than fascinating. Once you have children you may not be available to meet up with your friends as much as you did before, so they'll appreciate it if you retain your identity as a friend rather than a parent while you're with them. Bear in mind also that you'll meet other people with babies with whom you'll forge new friendships, based on the shared experience of new parenthood.

Your parents are about to become grandparents, so invite them in. Ask if they'd like to help you. It's also wise to listen to their views or you may be passing up good advice based on real experience. Many grandparents find it easier to have a relaxed and freer relationship with their grandchildren than they had with their own children, so take advantage of that.

You both know the personalities of the prospective grandparents however, and you may see difficulties ahead because their views and attitudes may not be the same as yours. You'll find later on that discussing with grandparents how you're going to set limits for your child is invaluable. It's also a good idea to agree that you'll both gently but firmly resist any attempt by them to interfere with your brand of parenting. That said, grandparents can be the bedrock on which the rest of the family stands, adding stability and encompassing strong and lasting

When to break the news

You might both want to tell everyone straightaway that you're having a baby; on the other hand you might want to hug your secret to yourselves for a while. You may surprise yourself at how it comes out, depending on who you're telling, because many people find admitting they're about to become parents to a third party seems to make it real for the first time. This is when the unqualified support of friends and family helps to overcome any feelings of doubt; alternatively you may find yourself confessing to your closest friend your ambivalence to the whole thing, even though on the surface you appear to be delighted. Once the news is out, bear in mind that in the event of a miscarriage, the more people you have told, the more distressing it may be for you if you have to explain that you've lost the baby. This is why many couples wait until the twelfth week before going public with the news.

"Many people find admitting to a third party they're about to become parents seems to make it real for the first time. This is when the unqualified support of friends and family helps."

relationships across the generations. Grandparents can be the cement that binds generations together and they offer that vital ingredient, caring interest, something your baby thrives on.

Before you break the news try to rehearse in advance what difference your pregnancy may make at work. You may never have clock-watched in your life before now, but it's difficult not to when you just want to get home and put your feet up. However, your colleagues, no matter how overjoyed for you, have the right to assume that you'll be as good value as you were before you got pregnant. If you can see possible pitfalls, be up front and negotiate. Before announcing you're pregnant to your boss, spend a little time thinking about when you are likely to want to go on maternity leave.

Although it's wonderful to be able to see your baby moving on the monitor's screen when you have your first scan, especially if you go together with your partner to the scan appointment, most women feel that bonding really begins once they feel their baby move. Though this may not happen until about 20 weeks in a first pregnancy, it's a landmark moment on your road to parenthood, so share your excitement and your feelings as much as possible with your partner and encourage him to feel your tummy as your baby moves – it will make your pregnancy even more real to him. The first sensations of movement often coincide with a change in energy levels, so you'll probably be feeling better about yourself and the baby than you ever thought possible at the start.

Being an expectant father is the one time in a man's life when he's quite likely to feel out of control. The feeling of being an outsider won't be helped by the way other people sometimes treat an expectant father: well-meaning female friends and relatives may unconsciously push him out of what they see as their territory. He may also find that the professionals, such as obstetricians and midwives, direct their conversations at you and not at him. To keep him really involved, try to direct people's comments to your partner too, especially when you meet together with health-care professionals.

Encourage him to bond with your bump too

It may be hard for him to bond with your bump but you can help him. This next bit is especially for him so suggest that he reads it, then talks to you about it.

Talk to your partner The best way to understand how your partner's feeling, and what's going on in her body, is to talk to her. Ask her what it feels like when the baby moves; discuss your plans for the birth together; find out if she's got particular discomforts that you can massage. She'll appreciate your interest.

Go to antenatal classes If you go to antenatal classes, you'll have an opportunity to learn about the birth and talk through your own concerns. This will help you to work out the best way to support your partner and enable you to be more involved in her birth choices and aware of the likely course of events during labour.

Encourage him to take the initiative and don't step back and allow your female relatives and friends to involve you more than him when he's around. Get him to tell his own friends and colleagues even though he may be subject to a certain amount of teasing but, equally, people may view him as more responsible and mature. Encourage him try to find out as much as he can about the pregnancy so that he can understand the changes taking place in your body. If possible, take him to the scans so that he can see your baby developing, talk about the fact that he's going to be a father and to ask as many questions as he wants.

Talk to other fathers Get to know the other expectant fathers at antenatal classes – they'll probably be feeling the same as you and be glad to have someone to talk to. Speak to friends and colleagues who have babies; find out about their experiences and ask their advice.

Read pregnancy and parenting books and any leaflets you're given. The more you understand about what's going on during the pregnancy, the more familiar it will become and it can help you to understand how your partner's feeling. It will enable you to ask the right questions. Websites are also a useful way of keeping yourself updated with information on pregnancy and parenting issues.

Ask questions Go to antenatal appointments with your partner so that you can meet the professionals and be present at diagnostic and screening tests. If you ask questions of professionals, they're more likely to talk to you as a couple and involve you both in the conversation. You will also learn from listening to other fathers' experiences.

The third trimester

Midwives are a crucial support for fathers so make sure you see your midwife together all through the third trimester. A midwife, for instance, can be the most important person in helping you and your partner become a confident and loving family when your newborn baby arrives. And from that a great deal follows.

We know that a child with an involved father – whether or not separated from the mother – will on average be financially better off, do better at school and be more likely to keep out of trouble. Your midwife can act as a kind of glue that strengthens your bond as parents as you navigate together the uncharted waters of pregnancy and the early days of parenthood.

Bond by doing everything together, discussing with your partner the type of birth that you want and deciding what his involvement will be. Encourage your partner to talk to his employer about taking time off to go to the antenatal appointments as well as to be with you at the birth, and to enable him to spend as much time as possible at home after the baby is born.

Chat about the issues raised by the birth plan you have compiled together and ask your partner for his views. If you feel strongly about certain issues, for example, you want to try for a drug-free labour, let him know how you feel so you can discuss the advantages and disadvantages together. Look forward to your partner being present at the birth and say so. It could bond the two of you together as nothing else can. Tell him that seeing the birth of your child is probably one of the most precious things he'll ever experience and holding your baby in the first seconds of life is proven to help with future bonding between father and child. Listen to Rob, 23, talking about the birth of his son, Ben, now four months old:

"The birth of your child is probably one of the most precious things he'll ever experience and holding your baby in the first seconds of life helps future bonding between father and child."

"I found the birth both terrifying and unbelievably moving. I felt as though I'd been punched below the belt. I cried as he came out and when I first held him in my arms. It was the realization that he was part of me. I want to give him a good life so that he can achieve anything he wants. I want him to be confident and successful in whatever he chooses."

As the children grow up, tasks like dealing with carers and teachers, taking and fetching from school, which used to be seen exclusively as a mother's responsibility, can be part of sharing care between mother and father. Most fathers recognize that being involved in their children's life and education is important, and they're fitting activities like the school run, helping in the classroom or taking their child to the doctor into their working day. It used to be accepted that mothers put the children to bed, but most fathers know that the bath and story routine is enjoyable, especially if they've been away from their children all day. The idea – prevalent not so long ago – that it was somehow demeaning for a man to push a pram is now laughable. Not only are men happy to be seen doing this, but they are usually also more than happy to take their children to the supermarket to do the weekly shopping with their partners. When deciding what kind of parents they'll be, most couples start out wanting to share parenting equally but few end up doing so.

Paternal bonding

You can never start bonding with your baby too early. Babies can hear sounds outside the womb by five or six months; if an expectant dad talks to his baby, the baby will bond to his voice while still in the womb and, in fact, can hear his low-pitched voice more clearly than his mother's. A man shouldn't feel awkward, he should think about the life he's created and love it. Help your partner bond with your baby by encouraging him to:

✳ **gently massage your tummy** and feel your baby move.

✳ **talk and coo softly to your baby,** and kiss and nuzzle your bump through your skin.

✳ **listen to the heartbeat using** a cardboard tube as a sound funnel.

✳ **go to scans with you** to see your baby develop.

Marcus Berkmann, in his book *Fatherhood*, describes how he developed a taste for being a hands-on father. He discovered a sense of freedom and that family actually makes men happy:

"Stay-at-home dads especially gain so much simply from spending vast amounts of time with their children. What you acquire as a stay-at-home father is the ability to look after kids and to know how they tick. You become able to cope with all the minutiae of their lives – which is all that matters for the moment. And the more attuned you become to them, the more satisfying the job becomes. Which is just as well, for although early parenthood is exhausting, maddening and at times atrociously boring, it is also – in its way – as vivid as life gets."

Popular culture embraces the dads who choose to be hands-on. In Nick Hornby's book *About a Boy*, a single man shrewdly and perhaps cynically fakes touchy-feely fatherhood to attract his love interest. The last few episodes of *Friends* had Ross, Chandler and Joey cooing over babies. And from *Neighbours* to *EastEnders*, soap opera men are no longer embarrassed to show affection for their children.

"Most fathers believe that being involved is important and they're fitting activities like the school run into their working day."

Being an involved dad can start as early as you like, and the earlier the better – during pregnancy listening to your baby's heartbeat and feeling him kick as he moves around in the womb, being present at your baby's birth and holding him in your arms for the first time, sharing the soothing rituals to get your baby sleeping through the night, as well as your baby's feeding, bathing and nappy-changing routines.

And baby makes three and somehow all the good intentions about equality in everything from decision-making to sharing the chores seem to fly out of the window once a baby arrives. That 50/50 partnership simply evaporates, says Susan Maushart in her book, *Wifework.*

Having a first child, Nora Ephron once remarked, is like throwing a hand grenade into a marriage. If that image seems harsh and dramatic the research tells us that much as we hope and plan otherwise, parenthood tends to exaggerate and harden gender differences within marriage, so husbands become more "husbandly" and wives more "wifely". Middle-class couples in their thirties and forties, where both partners have good jobs, seem to be most vulnerable to feeling the impact of a first baby.

Even the most wanted and loved first child sets off predictable changes in your relationship. You'll find that the division of domestic chores becomes "more traditional" and women go from doing most of it to doing almost all of it. Then the differences between you begin to show and grow. Next, satisfaction with your relationship and frequency of sex decline and finally affection, intimacy and friendship may dip.

The good news, however, is that marriages become stronger. One study found that the divorce rate among families with a pre-school child is half that of childless couples. When marriage partners become parents, they seem to stay together for longer. But the birth of a child entirely revamps the internal landscape of marriage according to leading family psychologist Judith Wallerstein. A new baby affects a woman much more than a man. For her it's a series of seismic

"The good news is that **marriages become stronger...** When marriage partners become parents they seem to **stay together for longer.**"

upheavals – it's a much more minor event for a man. A 20-year study of stable marriages found that three-quarters of fathers questioned were satisfied with their marriages during the years of childrearing, compared with only half of mothers.

This could be because motherhood changes a woman's core identity in many ways, some of which she doesn't expect. It also brings masses of extra work and juggling of responsibilities. New mothers who have done two to six times as much housework as their menfolk before the birth, find their workload increasing by between 50–90% after the birth. Much of this time is devoted to primary childcare, both hands-on and planning. Mothers are preoccupied by the baby's feeds, sleep, nappy-changing, clothing and minute-to-minute care and later on by childcare arrangements if and when they return to work.

Involving dads more in parenting Good though the new dad's intentions are, the time he spends on childcare is still little. Men do spend more time with their young families than they used to – two hours compared to 15 minutes 25 years ago. But most of the increase is concentrated on the fun bits – what researchers call "skimming off the cream" of parenthood. In Australia, for example, men do less than 20% of the childcare while they claim 40% of time spent playing with their kids. US research found that 70% of fathers weren't responsible for any childcare at all and only a fifth for one childcare task. One reason for this could be that fathers tend to work longer hours after the birth of their first child, possibly to avoid the new stresses that life with a baby brings.

Co-parenting isn't that easy. It means re-evaluating and making almost everything up as you go along. For new mothers whose creative energies are at a low ebb, caving in to traditional patterns of behaviour is sometimes easier than inventing new ones. You'll need to work at it together to make it work.

It's easier, too, to defer your sex life. US researchers Carolyn and Philip Cowan found lovemaking reaches an all-time low in the early months of parenthood after a decline in the last stages of pregnancy. A woman's sex drive is likely to remain low for several months after the birth. Sleep deprivation, the fallout from new parenthood can last not weeks, or months, but years. The struggle for sleep consumes the lives of most mothers and fathers can find themselves struggling for sex with those mothers. Recreating an intimate relationship after having a baby is a slow and gentle process that takes mutual understanding and time.

Babies don't differentiate between mum and dad

Babies and young children don't see any difference in male and female nurturing. They experience comfort, warmth and security from both adults and, though they soon learn to tell them apart, they don't make judgements aboutf what mothers' and fathers' roles ought to be.

Care for a child is indivisible – a baby will only compartmentalize his needs if this is what he learns from his experiences. Apart from breastfeeding, there is nothing a mother can do for a baby that can't be done by a father.

Babies don't need mothering and fathering, they need parenting. They need the most important adults in their lives to be models of what parents do for their children; when this is achieved, the next generation of fathers will not be at a loss as to what a father's role should be.

A new kind of parenting is evolving as the traditional family becomes a rarity and how it functions has been overhauled. Whereas fathers used to be wage-earners and protectors, having little direct involvement in day-to-day childcare, their importance as equal partners is now being recognized – side by side with women's increasing role as equal or even primary financial provider. The alternative family arrangement where the father cares for home and children by choice, while his partner earns the daily bread, is less unusual than in the past. One reason why such families are often strong and successful is that they take account of both partners' talents and are generally the result of careful discussion and planning. But whatever the practicalities of a family unit, providing an open, stable and loving environment in which to bring up children is probably the only important constant.

It's quite common for a pregnant woman or new mum to feel isolated nowadays. Many women postpone having children, and some decide against it altogether. You may find that you're the first in your social circle to start a family, and that you don't know any other pregnant women or fully-fledged mothers. It can be lonely. There's so much that you want to know and discuss. You may have little niggles and worries that you feel are too irrelevant or silly to talk about at your antenatal clinic, and you may wish that you knew someone who was going through the same thing or who already had a child. If so, find people to whom you can talk – join parent groups, approach other pregnant women in your childbirth classes, and ask your friends or family if they know any pregnant women, or parents with young children, whom you could get to know. These

"Whatever the practicalities of a family unit, an **open, stable and loving environment...** is probably the only important constant."

MIRIAM'S MAILBAG

Your questions answered

Q My partner's five-year-old son from a previous marriage lives
with us. How can I help him bond with his stepbrother?

This may look like a tough proposition fraught with all kinds of difficulties and,
to be honest with you, it can be unless you do one magical thing that will
ensure your two little boys will become firm friends: treat your little stepson in
exactly the same way as you treat you own child. First of all your partner will
love you for it and your relationship will go from strength to strength. Secondly,
you'll be acting as a role model for your own son and with each of your kind
actions towards your stepson you're saying to him in effect, this is how you
treat your little brother. And by the way don't call him stepbrother nor call
yourself stepmother. He's your son's brother and you are his mother to all
intents and purposes. The key is to be even-handed. So don't make any
differences between them, don't favour one over the other, treat them similarly
in every way, as you would two brothers. Try especially to be fair if there are
any conflicts and if you think your son has been selfish, cruel, spiteful, don't
hesitate to tell him so and of course do the same with your stepson. On the
other hand, be quick to praise both your son for being kind and affectionate
and your stepson for being brave and trying hard. All of you are secure enough
to take care of yourselves except your stepson, so look out for him.

Q I'm worried that I will have to change my lifestyle completely
when my baby arrives. Do I have to give up everything when
I'm a mum?

No, you don't have to give everything up. But you'll find that you give up a lot
of things you've held dear for many years quite willingly. I encourage you not

to think of the changes you have to make because you're a mum as "giving up" cherished activities. That isn't a positive way to look at your new life, especially when the changes will bring you so much joy.

The most helpful approach is to think of changes as trade-offs. So for instance you might trade off clubbing for spending an hour at the mother and baby club watching your baby play and chatting to other mothers. Or you might give up having a glass of wine with your lunch or dinner in exchange for eating lots of healthy food so that your breast milk will nourish your baby. While you're breastfeeding you are the sole source of nourishment for your growing baby and for most women that is enormously satisfying. It justifies their whole existence. And you can also come to an arrangement with your partner that you share babycare so that you can have time out – an evening with the girls once a week, a half day at the hairdresser and looking around the shops, and a babysitter for an evening so that you can both go out. It's a big step changing from a couple to a family but the rewards are greater than anything else you've ever done in your lives before.

Q Will my partner be entitled to paternity leave?

A man is entitled to take two weeks' paid paternity leave following the birth of a new baby, provided he is the biological father or the mother's partner with responsibility for bringing up the child. He must have been working for his current employer for a minimum of 26 weeks by the 15th week before the baby is due and he must also give his employer 28 days' notice of when he would like his paternity leave to start. Advance warning of your partner's plans for paternity leave will be appreciated by his employer.

relationships may provide support long after your baby is born. Don't forget your partner either – if you're feeling isolated, he probably is too, so talk to him, include him, and expand your social circle together.

Your sensuality and your baby are important. Fathers-to-be may recoil from sex lest they hurt their partner and their unborn baby. They needn't. Neither will come to any harm. Indeed, the opposite is true.

You may find sex more exciting and satisfying than ever. In fact, a woman will sometimes achieve orgasm or multiple orgasms for the first time when she is

Sex is good for bonding

Good sex in pregnancy is very enjoyable, and it helps to prepare you for childbirth by keeping your pelvic muscles strong and supple. It also bonds you closer to your partner, which will help you cope much better with the stresses to come.

There is absolutely no physical reason why a woman having a normal pregnancy shouldn't enjoy sexual relations with her partner to the full, and sex needn't stop any earlier than the onset of labour, both partners being willing. In a low-risk pregnancy, the uterine spasms that accompany orgasms are perfectly safe, and in late pregnancy may be beneficial because they help prepare the uterus for the rigours of labour.

There's no question, however, that extremely athletic sex isn't a good idea, because it may cause

pregnant. This enhanced sexuality is principally because of the high levels of female hormones and pregnancy hormones that circulate throughout her body when she is expecting.

One of the effects of the rise in oestrogen levels during pregnancy is an increase in blood flow, especially in the vagina and its folds and the labia which become slightly stretched and swollen. This stretching and swelling make the nerve endings hypersensitive, resulting in rapid arousal of the clitoris and the vagina. The vaginal secretions are quite profuse, penetration is particularly easy and a climax can be achieved quite quickly if the clitoris is stimulated simultaneously.

soreness and abrasions and a pregnant woman should of course be free of these unnecessary discomforts.

In the early months you can use any position you choose, but as your abdomen swells you may find some lovemaking positions uncomfortable. After about 24 weeks it's not advisable to lie on your back for any length of time so avoid the missionary position, with your partner on top – there are plenty of other exciting positions. Also, these alternatives are often the best positions to use when you resume lovemaking after the birth.

Don't worry if the missionary position becomes awkward because there are several other positions that will enhance your enjoyment – without in any way diminishing that of your partner. Side-by-side positions are good as are rear-entry positions, because your abdomen isn't under any pressure from the weight of your partner. Sitting positions are particularly enjoyable in the later months of pregnancy, and enable you to adjust your position but still see your partner's face and feel close to him.

The intensity of orgasm may reach new heights and the time taken to "come down" from an orgasm can be greatly extended. This is evident in the labia minora which can remain swollen for anything up to two hours after orgasm, particularly in the last trimester. If you enjoy sex, your baby does too. Your baby savours all the pleasant sensations you feel. The pregnancy hormones which pour out during sex are good for the placenta and for your baby's health.

Pregnancy tends to accentuate your personality. If you're a placid person you'll tend to stay calm and laid back. If you're a livewire you'll tend to be more active than ever – till fatigue reins you in. If you're of a nervous disposition it's possible that you'll panic when faced with the unexpected. It's useful to know how you may change during pregnancy because it has given you the chance to put in place some safeguards to keep you mentally resilient.

One of the most potentially difficult aspects of pregnancy to deal with is that your partner can never know what it feels like to be pregnant. For you pregnancy is very much an internal experience; for your partner it's all external. So he can never feel what you feel. His emotions can't match yours. But that doesn't mean you can't explain them to him. Try to because it draws him in instead of shutting him out. That way he'll be more understanding and sympathetic about any and all of the difficulties you face and the worries you have. The strongest weapon you have to stay emotionally stable is to bond together as a parental team so you can split domestic life down the middle from day one of your pregnancy. You can do all the planning together whether it's financial, the birth plan, how much maternity and paternity leave you'll take, attending antenatal appointments together or fitting

"Keep talking together. You need each other more now than ever before. Denying or ignoring your fears or feelings won't make them go away."

Talking is great too

It's natural to talk and share what you're feeling and thinking during your pregnancy. Your partner is the logical first choice, and will probably be anxious to talk to you. There are bound to be things that he would like to talk about: worries, things that he may have refrained from discussing with you because he thought that he might upset you or you might think him silly, or because you were too busy, or too tired. Keep talking. You need each other more now than ever before. Denying or ignoring your fears and feelings won't make them go away. Suppressed feelings have a very nasty way of festering and then surfacing when you are least equipped to deal with them, thus becoming full-blown problems. You should be able to avoid these issues if you bring them out in the open when they first occur and then get on with your lives.

antenatal classes into your diaries so you both can attend. You can also get some baby practice by visiting together friends who have babies. You watch, learn and start getting used to handling small babies then comparing notes when you return home. That's a very bonding experience. You might like to invite some new parents to your home for a meal where the topic is to be solely babies. What happened? How did they cope? What were their feelings? That way you shoehorn yourselves into the idea of being parents and prepare yourself for the life-changing event of having a baby in the house. This team-baby will be working smoothly by the time your baby arrives and will continue to in the weeks and months after the birth, better able to deal with the ups and downs of being a threesome rather than a twosome.

Your questions answered

Q My partner and I would like to go away on holiday before our baby is born but we're not sure if it's safe to fly and whether there are particular destinations we should avoid?

Travelling by plane isn't a good idea after your seventh month because of pressure changes in the cabin. If you really want to fly at this time check with the airline about whether they'll need to see a doctor's letter before letting you on the plane. Try to sit towards the front of the plane and you'll feel less travel-sick. Don't fly in small private planes that have unpressurized cabins. Always eat lightly and make sure you empty your bladder before you go onboard. Buckle your seat belt low on your hips.

You really shouldn't travel any distance from home in the last couple of months. You need to be close to your maternity unit should your labour come on early. What I'd really recommend is having a weekend away quite close to home if there's only a month or so to go. Leave plenty of time for your journey and travel in short bursts rather than a long stretch. Carry a drink such as milk or fruit juice in a flask. Have some glucose sweets to prevent nausea and wear an eye mask and ear plugs so that you can sleep when travelling.

Q I have a very successful career but have always wanted children. What are the issues I should consider before returning to work after the birth? If I do return to work will my baby bond with his caregiver rather than me?

Think carefully about when you want to go back to work after your baby is born and what you'll do when you return. You may want to go back under different working conditions and you'll need to talk to your employer about this. For

example you might want to try working part-time or doing a job share or flexi-work or some freelance activity that allows you to work from home. Bear in mind that both you and your partner are entitled to take a year's extra parental leave (unpaid) during your child's first year provided you've worked for your employer for at least a year. If you've agreed between you that one of you will go back to work and the other partner will care for the baby at home, the carer needs a lot of support especially in the early days. Always try to share the responsibilities. Don't assume your partner will sort out the problems or be the one to cope when, say, your baby is ill. If you're both working share the household jobs and the daily routine including collecting your baby from the childminder or getting home first to take over from the nanny. Far from being a chore, these precious moments alone with your baby will be something you come to cherish. Arranging childcare is of the utmost importance. Work out a routine for expressing your milk if you're breastfeeding and you may have to continue to do this at the office. There's no way that your baby will bond with his caregiver instead of bonding with you. You are the love of his life and he knows you from all others.

Q I want to build a good support network for myself locally as I don't live close to my parents. Where's the best place to start?
Joining a local antenatal group is a great way to meet other parents-to-be. You will find that going through something as life-changing as pregnancy will bind you to new friends in similar situations and this will form the basis of your support network. Your GP, your midwife and other healthcare professionals know of organizations local to you to meet any specific needs you may have.

how I affect my unborn baby

Your unborn baby inhabits your body; her entire world is you. For nine months your body is your baby's body. So close is **your blood** to your baby's blood that **only one cell separates you.** Everything from the food you eat to the **music you enjoy** is part of your baby's experience too.

You'll never be as close to your baby again All that's good and healthy in your body – hormones, proteins, carbohydrates, vitamins like folic acid, minerals like calcium and iron, vital nutrients like essential fatty acids, brain chemicals that make you happy like endorphins, serotonin and dopamine – benefit your baby too because you share them.

It follows all that's not so healthy also passes through you to your baby – alcohol, drugs, medication, some bacteria, some viruses (rubella) and stress hormones such as cortisol. Even when your body overheats, your raised body temperature becomes your baby's raised temperature too. You are indivisible from your baby for nine months. So you can appreciate that one of the most powerful ways to bond with your baby is to take control of your diet in order to make sure she is getting everything she needs for healthy development.

What my baby learns from me

Think of your body as the environment your baby grows, develops and lives in. You and your baby are more interdependent than you think. Physically, you are inseparable. Even at a few weeks from conception your baby starts adapting to the environment you're creating in your body. So your growing baby takes cues and messages from you and uses them to predict the environment she is likely to live in after birth. Your clever baby starts adjusting and adapting her development and metabolism to give her the best chance of survival in the environment she anticipates in the world outside the womb. The scientific term for this behaviour is Predictive Adaptive Responses (PARs).

Your baby's wellbeing
depends on your diet

Let's say you're eating irregularly and your blood sugar level keeps dropping low. Your baby is short of glucose too so she responds by conserving as much as she can. She decides times are going to be tough so first she makes sure her all-important brain doesn't go without by raising the level of sugar in the blood going to her brain. But this means other organs inevitably go short.

Organs such as muscles go short, so they don't develop as they should. Insulin (which lowers blood sugar) is damped down to keep what little sugar there is circulating in your baby's blood. If low blood sugar is a permanent feature of your pregnancy your baby will be thin, poorly muscled and of low birth weight.

This doesn't matter if your baby has got her predictions of life after birth right. She has adapted perfectly. The problems arise when her development doesn't match her life after birth. I'm sure you'll do everything possible to feed your newborn baby well and if you do your baby will find she is not equipped to deal with such a rich diet when she has modelled her metabolism for leaner times. Her prediction of the times ahead, deduced from the nutritional environment she experienced in the womb, turns out to be inaccurate. This in turn leads to the risk that she might become a fat toddler, an obese child and an adult in danger of developing heart disease and diabetes. The size of the risk depends on how badly

"Your growing baby takes cues and messages from you and uses them to predict the environment she is likely to live in after birth."

your baby got it wrong, the size of the mismatch between the environment she predicted in the womb and the one she actually finds herself in. You can see that the baby who is poorly nourished in the womb but grows up eating sugary, high-fat, high-calorie foods will be at high risk of obesity, diabetes and heart disease.

I believe therefore that it's always wrong to diet during pregnancy. A developing baby needs and must have a surfeit of all the nutrients she requires to grow healthily in the womb so that she can make the right predictions about her future diet and lower her risk of disease by developing a metabolism that is designed to cope with the food she will eat once she is born. If during your pregnancy you cut down on healthy food like carbs, proteins, fruit, vegetables, healthy fats like omega-3, your baby's body won't learn how to handle and process these foods in the future.

Two professors of paediatric nutrition, Professor Gluckman in New Zealand and Professor Hanson in Southampton, believe that this scenario explains why we're living with an epidemic of Type 2 diabetes, where diets in the West are becoming ever richer in the wrong kind of nutrients while a baby's development in the womb is constrained by poor nutrition, particularly if you smoke.

Your baby responds fast to your diet. The frightening aspect of this discovery is that it can happen so quickly. Your baby makes rapid, short-term changes in the womb which result in diseases in only a few years because the baby inside you is sensitive to the environment you create from the moment

"A developing baby needs and must have a surfeit of all the **nutrients she requires to grow healthily** in the womb so she can make the right predictions about her future diet and **lower her risk of disease.**"

Your baby's needs

Every calorie, vitamin, or gram of protein that your baby needs must be eaten by you. You are the sole manager of your unborn child's nutrition; you, and only you, can make sure that the best quality food reaches her.

You will fulfil all of your baby's requirements if you eat lots of fresh fruit, vegetables, beans, peas, wholemeal cereals, fish, fowl, and low-fat dairy products. A Danish study has shown that eating oil-rich fish – fresh tuna, salmon, herring, sardines, mackerel – once a week may help lessen the risk of pre-term birth. Make your diet as varied as possible, choosing from a wide range of foodstuffs.

A diet rich in protein lifts serotonin levels for you and your baby, so small changes to your lifestyle and diet are very worthwhile. Stick to these lifestyle changes and gradually they become a way of life and have a dramatic effect on your baby's long-term wellbeing.

of fertilization. This presents a compelling case for meticulous and unceasing care over your diet and the overall health of your body during pregnancy. Your optimal health goes a long way to ensuring that your baby will grow up to be at a lower risk of developing diseases as an adult. For if your baby's adult appetite, food preferences, tendency to store fat and desire to exercise are all predetermined in your womb and at a very early stage, then changing your child's lifestyle later in life may be too late to have any real effect. It's a mandate for you to follow in order to be at your healthiest during your pregnancy.

But don't forget mum

The other important person you must eat for during pregnancy is, of course, you. A good diet will mean that you have better reserves to cope with, and recover from, the indisputable strain of pregnancy and the hard physical work of labour.

Anaemia and pre-eclampsia are much more common in those mothers who have a poor diet, and some problems, such as morning sickness and leg cramps, may be exacerbated by what you do or don't eat – not eating enough salt, for example, can mean you experience leg cramps.

Overall, good nutrition will help minimize excessive mood swings, fatigue and many common complaints. In addition, a sensible eating regime that cuts out or restricts the amount of empty calories you consume will mean that you will be left with less excess fat to lose after your child has been born.

You're a feeding tube to your baby because everything a mother eats filters down through the umbilical cord, explains Keith Godfrey of the University of Southampton's medical school's research unit, who does a lot of work on foetal and infant nutrition.

See yourself, literally, as a feeding tube for your baby. If you have an iron, iodine or folic-acid deficiency during your pregnancy, these deficiencies will be passed on to your baby with potentially damaging results. Your iron deficiency may inhibit your baby's growth and impair his immunity, so eat iron-rich foods like spinach and ask your midwife about iron tablets. A lack of iodine may result in cretinism, which is characterized by dwarfism and mental retardation – seafood, seaweed (such as kelp and nori), eggs, meat and dairy products are good sources of iodine.

While folic acid is necessary for healthy neural tube development and is added as a supplement to many commercially produced cereals and breads, you must also take it in tablet form for the first four months of pregnancy to get your daily requirement of 400 mcg.

Your baby's brain is modelled by what you eat, and there is now more evidence to show how diet affects the unborn baby. One vital piece of nutritional advice to emerge recently is the benefit of certain omega-3 fats for the developing baby. Scientists have been studying the importance of the omega-3 fatty acid, DHA (docosahexaenoic acid), and have found that it has an important role to play in healthy brain and eye development.

DHA omega-3 is referred to as a polyunsaturated essential fatty acid, which the body needs but can't produce in adequate amounts by itself. Instead we rely on our diet to make up the difference. Significantly, evidence suggests that the diet of pregnant women in the West probably contains less than a quarter of the recommended intake of DHA.

DHA is important because it's a vital building block for the healthy development of membranes in the eye, brain and nervous system. For this reason, adequate levels of DHA are particularly crucial during the explosive growth spurts within the second half of pregnancy and during the first year of life. Babies can't produce their own DHA at this stage so rely on their mother's dietary intake.

Studies have shown that infants who have access to higher levels of DHA while in the womb have a whole range of health benefits including better

"Babies can't produce their own DHA at this stage so rely on their mother's dietary intake... It's a vital building block for healthy development."

hand–eye co-ordination, sharper vision, higher IQ and possibly a lower risk of heart disease in later life. Emerging studies also show that DHA may help women carry their babies to a healthy term, reducing the risk of pre-term birth. In a trial of women receiving a DHA supplement during the third trimester, the average length of pregnancy increased by six days. Research has also revealed low levels of DHA and red blood cells in women with postnatal depression, leading some scientists to believe that increasing a mother's level of DHA could protect her emotional wellbeing after pregnancy and also possibly prevent the onset of postnatal depression in the first place.

So what are the best sources? The best known rich source of DHA is oily fish – salmon, trout, fresh tuna, mackerel, herring, sardines and pilchards. Alongside the increased awareness of the nutritional value of these cold-water sea fish, there have been warnings about mercury levels in some oily fish. For this reason the UK Food Standards Agency recommends that pregnant women limit their consumption of oily fish to one portion a week but to eat other fish ad lib.

For non-fish eaters, the British Nutrition Foundation recommends taking DHA supplements from microalgae, the original source of DHA in oily fish (fish eat microalgae that contain DHA and then become a DHA source). A certain amount of DHA is also found in eggs from hens fed on algae or flax seeds. Alternatively, linseed, rapeseed and flaxseed oil are examples of supplementary sources of DHA, as are walnuts and tofu – and all are suitable for vegetarians.

"... some scientists believe that increasing a mother's level of DHA could **protect her emotional wellbeing** after pregnancy and possibly prevent the **onset of postnatal depression...** "

Some foods to avoid

In order to safeguard your health and that of your baby while you are pregnant it's best that you avoid the following foods:

✳ **Unpasteurized milk and dairy products,** some soft cheeses, ready-prepared coleslaw, pate, cooked-chilled foods and meat that hasn't been properly cooked as all these foods can contain large numbers of listeria bacteria.

✳ **Meat that hasn't been properly cooked** – toxoplasmosis can be picked up by eating raw or undercooked pork or steak; salmonella can be picked up by eating undercooked chicken. The cooking process destroys the bacteria.

✳ **Shellfish** It's best not to eat raw shellfish when you're pregnant. This will reduce your chances of getting food poisoning which is not something you want to contend with at any time, especially when you're pregnant. You should also avoid eating shark, swordfish and marlin as these may contain high levels of mercury.

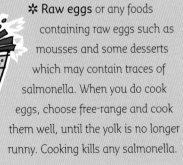

✳ **Raw eggs** or any foods containing raw eggs such as mousses and some desserts which may contain traces of salmonella. When you do cook eggs, choose free-range and cook them well, until the yolk is no longer runny. Cooking kills any salmonella.

Super fruit and vegetables for you and your baby

By eating these foods on a regular basis you are guaranteeing a continuous flow of vital nutrients to your developing baby. You are also providing your own body with the fuel it needs to stay fit and well and to carry your baby safely and healthily to term.

* **Broccoli contains lots of calcium** but also a great selection of antioxidants, particularly one called sulphoraphane, as well as vitamin C, beta-carotene, quercetin, glutathione and lutein. It's also one of the richest food sources of the trace metal chromium, which is essential for healthy red blood cells. Chromium prevents insulin resistance and helps normalize blood sugar.

* **Carrots are a must every day** – all that fibre fights off sluggish bowels plus carrots are full of beta-carotene for vitamin A.

* **Grapes contain 20 known antioxidants** mainly in the skin and seeds – the more colourful the skin, the greater the antioxidant effect. Three glasses of purple grape juice daily helps to keep your blood thin and your blood pressure down – always good in pregnancy. Raisins are even more potent than fresh grapes.

* **The darker the berry** the more antioxidants it has, so go for blueberries which have an antioxidant called anthocyanin. Both blueberries and cranberries help ward off urinary tract infections. Strawberries and all berries are rich in the antioxidant vitamin C.

* **Citrus fruits** Oranges contain a vast array of antioxidants, including carotenoids, terpenes, flavonoids and vitamin C. Grapefruit has a unique type

of fibre, especially in the membranes and the juice sacs, so perhaps you could include citrus fruits in your breakfast each day.

✳ **Tomatoes contain lypocene** which preserves mental and physical functioning. Cooking and canning tomatoes doesn't destroy lycopene but it does destroy vitamin C. Cooking tomatoes liberates the lycopene.

✳ **Cabbage is high in antioxidants** and fibre. Cabbage eaters have a lower risk of breast cancer. Savoy cabbage is the most potent.

✳ **Red and yellow onions are rich** in quercetin which keeps arteries healthy.

"A sensible eating regime that cuts out or restricts the amount of empty calories you consume will mean that you'll be left with less excess fat to lose after your child is born."

✳ **Avocado contains one of the most** potent antioxidants. Though avocados contain lots of fat, it's healthy fat in that it lowers blood cholesterol. Avocados contain potassium to protect blood vessels.

✳ **Spinach is rich in iron**, essential for you and your baby and it may protect against high blood pressure and even psychiatric problems because of its powerful antioxidant lutein.

Shaping your baby's
taste for food

Have you ever wondered why Mexican babies grow up with a liking for Mexican food, Indian babies for Indian food, Chinese babies for Chinese food and so on? The answer is that mothers teach their babies what tastes and flavours to like while they're still in the womb. Mothers then confirm these tastes and flavours through what they eat while they're breastfeeding. Let me explain.

 The flavours of many foods pass into your blood during and following digestion and make their way across the placenta to your baby's circulation. Your baby passes these flavours out in its urine into the amniotic fluid. Your baby swallows mouthfuls of amniotic fluid from time to time and will, for the first time, taste and savour the flavours in the food that you eat. A baby's sense of taste is quite well developed by 14 weeks and after that you can "train" your baby to acquire a taste for healthy foods by eating them yourself. If you want to avoid mealtime tussles with your child over broccoli make sure you eat plenty during your pregnancy and again while breastfeeding. Babies interpret anything they taste in breastmilk as good for them and they want more. You can make your milk taste "green" by eating lots of salads, leaves and vegetables.

"We might stem those toddler mealtime fights over certain foods if we introduced our children to a wide variety of fruit and vegetables while still in the womb. Wouldn't that be a bonus?"

Your baby's food preferences are formed early. There's good research showing your baby acquires food preferences in the womb. There are even ultrasound scans showing a baby "sipping" the amniotic fluid to sample a taste she likes. In one study, three groups of mums-to-be were given a daily glass of either broccoli or carrot juice, while a control group received only water. Later, when their infants were introduced to solids, the babies ate more cereal when it was mixed with whichever juice their pregnant mothers had drunk, expressing their preference for a taste remembered from the womb.

So while you are eating a healthy diet during your pregnancy you may well also be shaping your baby's preferences for healthy foods in her later life, setting her up with a palate that automatically opts for healthy over unhealthy, variety over monotony.

Think before you...

... choose drinks during pregnancy. Do you know how it will impact on your baby's activity in the womb? When you drink coffee, even if it's decaf, your baby's breathing and heart rate change because of the number of chemicals in coffee. One measure of vodka can affect your baby's breathing for up to half an hour within three to 30 minutes of you drinking it, even though your blood–alcohol level is quite low.

... smoke or take recreational drugs that have side-effects and can have serious consequences not only for you but also for your baby. Think of the long-term implications for you both. Check first with your pharmacist about over-the-counter drugs and always read the label. Even some over-the-counter cold remedies are not advised during pregnancy, so it's wise to check first.

"Statistics reported at a San Francisco conference recently showed that having fish even once a week reduced the number of cases of eczema in children at the age of five by nearly half."

What you eat can even protect your baby from allergies in childhood. You can do so much for your baby's health by eating the right sorts of foods in the right quantities. What you eat affects your baby's long-term health, not just infant health. In terms of your developing baby's healthy growth it's imperative you take 400mcg of folic acid every day for the first four months because you probably won't get enough from food alone.

Recent research from Aberdeen says that a high intake of foods rich in zinc such as bran, nuts, eggs, shellfish and vitamins D (oily fish, butter, eggs) and E (seeds, broccoli, egg yolk) during pregnancy can lower the chances of asthma and allergic diseases in your baby as she grows up.

Eating plenty of fish and apples during pregnancy can actually improve your child's lung function and reduce the likelihood of asthma. Statistics reported at a San Francisco conference recently showed that having fish even once a week reduced the number of cases of eczema in children at the age of five by nearly half. The same study showed that if you eat four apples a week during pregnancy your baby will be a third less likely to be wheezy in early childhood and half as likely to have asthma. All this knowledge available from research is such a bonus – you can choose to eat foods that promote health in your baby.

How exercise helps
your baby – and you

Pregnancy puts a strain on your body so the fitter you are, the better you'll cope. Your fitness ascends to a higher level than you've ever known in terms of stamina and strength. The stronger your core, girdle and limb muscles get before you're pregnant and in the first trimester, the more able they are to take the strain of your overworked lower back ligaments which start to soften up during pregnancy so that your joints can expand to let the baby out.

As you gain more weight and your tummy becomes bigger you may try to make up for the extra weight on the front by leaning backwards. This throws your head back so that your line of vision is different from usual. Your centre of gravity is also altered so you become unsteady and may find that you bump into things or drop them. Pregnancy causes a softening and relaxation of the ligaments of the pelvic joints so that there's quite a strain on your spine at the back. This loosening and increased mobility of the joints is necessary in order to allow your baby to be born through your pelvic outlet. However it causes backache, so sit with a straight back, don't wear high-heeled shoes and preferably sit on a hard chair or the floor. Always bend with a straight back or if lifting, bend the knees and lift from the crouching position. Avoid lifting altogether if you possibly can.

Maintaining a good posture will help you minimize backache and fatigue that increases as your pregnancy advances. Your enlarging abdomen thrusts your centre of gravity forward and because of this you arch your back backwards, putting your back muscles under constant strain, hence the backache. When you're standing, sitting or walking with the correct posture your neck and back should be in a straight line.

Exercise is good for you...

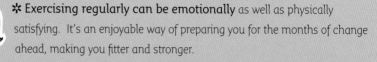

❋ **Exercising regularly can be emotionally** as well as physically satisfying. It's an enjoyable way of preparing you for the months of change ahead, making you fitter and stronger.

❋ **You'll receive an emotional lift** from the release of hormones like endorphins after you have exercised and you will feel a de-stressing effect as the release of tranquillizing hormones after exercise helps you to relax and wind down.

❋ **You can improve your self-awareness** as you learn how to use your body in new ways. Breathing exercises are particularly helpful as they make you focus in hard on how your body works.

❋ **You can alleviate backache,** leg cramp, constipation, and breathlessness by regular exercise.

"Maintaining a good posture will help you minimize backache and fatigue... your neck and back should be in a straight line."

❋ **You meet other mums at antenatal exercise classes** and can even share your exercise routine with your partner so you both benefit. As a result of taking exercise, your energy levels will increase and you'll have more physical and mental strength and stamina for the work of labour.

❋ **You'll regain your shape more quickly after delivery,** especially if regular exercise has been a feature of your pregnancy and you continue to exercise as soon as is wise after delivery.

...and good for your baby

✳ **Every time you exercise within your limit,** your baby gets a surge of oxygen into her blood that sets her metabolism alight and gives her a real high. All her tissues, especially her brain, function on top form and receive a real boost from the extra oxygen.

✳ **The hormones that are released during your exercise** pass across the placenta and reach your baby. At the beginning of exercise, therefore, your baby receives an emotional lift from your adrenaline.

✳ **During exercise, your baby also experiences** the powerful effect of endorphins, our own natural morphine-like substances released while exercising, that make us feel extremely good, happy and positive.

✳ **The motion of exercise is extremely soothing** and is good for your baby as she feels comforted by the rocking movements. She will respond positively to soothing, rocking movements when she is a newborn baby so it's a great idea to get her used to the feeling early on in pregnancy.

✳ **As you exercise, your abdominal muscles** exert a kind of massage on your baby that's comforting and soothing.

✳ **During exercise, blood flow is optimum** and so your baby's growth and development proceeds apace with all its benefits.

✳ **After exercise, endorphins** have a profound tranquillizing effect that can last up to eight hours and your baby also experiences this.

If you relax, your
baby relaxes too

Good relaxation techniques combine the release of tension in the mind and body with deep, regular breathing, and it's helpful to practise these techniques so that towards the end of pregnancy they've become second nature.

A good way to relax your whole body completely is to use the tense and relax technique. It's a pleasant way to relax during pregnancy and is good preparation for labour, when it's a great help to be able to relax most of your muscles so that your uterus contracts in isolation, without the rest of your body tensing.

When you relax, by whatever means, when you slow down your breathing and concentrate on long, gradual exhalation, when you close your eyes and visualize a beautiful scene, or when you empty your mind and think of black velvet, your brain waves change to alpha waves that normalize all your organs and bring you a deep feeling of calm. Your pulse rate slows and your blood pressure drops – very good for your baby.

This feeling is engendered by brain hormones which calm down the fear and anxiety centres in the brain. Your own stress response with stress hormones dies away. These calming hormones, such as serotonin, dopamine, oxytocin and prolactin, inhibit your baby's stress response and keep her stress hormone levels low. So your baby feels your calmness, your tranquillity, your love. She feels rewarded. Your baby's brain actually grows in a different, healthy way as a result. It will develop circuits and chemical connections that protect it from stress and equip it to better deal with stress after it's born, patterns which will serve for the whole of your baby's life. All this, when you relax and breathe deeply.

Tense and relax technique

This technique involves tensing and relaxing different parts of your body in sequence. Your partner can help by touching you where he can see you're tensing up: you respond to his touch by relaxing. Practise twice a day for 15–20 minutes if you can, before meals or an hour or more after eating.

❋ **Find a comfortable position** either lying on your back or propped up with cushions. Close your eyes and then try to clear your mind of any stressful thoughts, anxieties or worries by breathing in and out slowly and regularly and concentrating all your attention on your breathing actions.

❋ **Let pleasant thoughts flow through your head,** and if any worrying or nagging thought tries to recur, prevent it from doing so by saying "no" under your breath, then return to concentrating completely on your deep breathing.

❋ **When your mind is totally relaxed** and your breathing deep and regular, you can begin the tense and relax routine. Talk your baby through it.

❋ **Think about your right hand:** tense it for a moment, palm upward, then relax it and tell it to feel heavy and warm. Work up through the right side of your body, tensing and relaxing your forearm, upper arm, and your shoulder.

❋ **Repeat the process** on the upper left side of your body. Next, roll your knees outwards, and then in turn tense and relax your buttocks, thighs, calves and your feet. Press your lower back gently into the floor, then release.

❋ **Finally relax the muscles of your head and neck.** Relax the muscles of your face, eyes, and forehead, and smooth away any frowns.

❋ **Ask your baby if it felt good.**

Your questions answered

Q Can you explain why you advise not drinking any alcohol during pregnancy? I have read many conflicting theories on the subject and would appreciate some clear guidance.

On this thorny question the medical authorities seem not able to make up their minds. In May of 2007 the Department of Health advised pregnant women and those trying to conceive to try and cut out alcohol altogether rather than limit it. Now, the National Institute of Clinical Excellence (NICE) has produced draft guidance stating that pregnant women can consume up to 1.5 units of alcohol (a small glass) a day after the first three months of pregnancy. Their reasons are that there's no consistent evidence to show that a small amount of alcohol damages unborn children.

A British Medical Association (BMA) report concluded this year that heavy drinking by pregnant women can cause learning and physical disabilities and behavioural problems in their children. The BMA said that such disorders can only be prevented by abstaining completely from alcohol during pregnancy and were concerned that any relaxation could be misinterpreted.

The experts have concluded that there's no consistent evidence of a harmful effect of low to moderate intake of alcohol during pregnancy but neither is the evidence strong enough to rule out any risk. It's that last line that bothers me. I've always advocated not drinking at all while pregnant because we don't know how sensitive any unborn baby is to the toxic effect of alcohol. Alcohol is a poison to a baby and, yes, in order to have an effect on a baby of the magnitude of Foetal Alcohol Syndrome a woman has to be a moderate drinker or worse. But why take the risk? It just seems to me a no-brainer. And all for what? The odd glass of wine with a questionable effect.

Q I understand that my baby loves listening to music. Are there specific types of music that babies like?

Yes, there are. The type of music a baby likes is any music she hears while inside her mother's womb. I have a daughter-in-law who's a singer with a rich contralto voice and she's also a music teacher. One Christmas, before my granddaughter was born, my daughter-in-law had to rehearse the school choir for three months singing Christmas carols. After my granddaughter was born she would go to sleep very quickly if we played a CD of Christmas carols to her. She learned, memorized and took comfort from the music she heard while in the womb and remembered the lovely feelings of warmth and security that accompanied hearing the music.

I guess what you're referring to is the fabled, yet disputed, Mozart Effect – a theory stating that baroque music increases brain activity more effectively than other kinds of music. The Mozart Effect, though first described as a theory in 1991, only really surfaced in 1993 when a US psychologist and a physicist at the Univeristy of California reported that brief exposure to a Mozart piano sonata could raise an IQ score eight to nine points. A New York Times piece in 1994 extrapolated their findings to "listening to Mozart actually makes you smarter". This claim has been undermined by subsequent studies. But it hasn't stopped a slew of products like Baby Mozart and Mozart for Babies with an implied claim that they will promote, among other things, the development of logical thinking and mathematical ability. For parents wanting to do the best for their babies it has purchase appeal though I beg you to be cautious because the benefits are unproven.

Meditation

I'd like to tell you a personal anecdote that describes the power of positive thought. One of my daughters-in-law was expecting twins and she was alerted to the possibility of twin-to-twin transfusion when one twin siphons off the lion's share of blood leaving the other twin undernourished and undersized.

At one of her antenatal visits she was told this appeared to be happening and one of the twins was smaller than the other. She immediately gave this twin a name and at intervals through the day she would talk to her, encouraging her, telling her to keep fighting, keep growing, saying how much she was loved and how everyone wanted her to be born safely. When the twins were born she was a pound heavier than her sister and has kept this lead throughout her first year.

Was this the power of positive thought because her mother spent time every day concentrating on her, cheering her on, telling her how much she longed for her to be born and share her life with her dad and big sister? Did my daughter-in-law empower her baby for growth and survival in the womb? Did she, through her imagination, will her daughter in the womb to grow so much that she overtook her twin sister? Did my daughter-in-law, by visualizing her ailing twin as a healthy, bouncing baby actually make her that way? I don't know. I'm unaware of any good science that would back up this one-off experiment. And while I'm sceptical of any anecdotal evidence I'm inclined to think my daughter-in-law worked her extraordinary magic. Whether that's true or not what she did by reaching out each day to her unborn daughter through her feelings, her imagination and her emotions was to form an unbreakably strong bond with her. This has made my daughter-in-law an exceptional mother and her twin baby a relaxed, outgoing, cheery little girl. She and her mother shared secret

Thinking and writing

Keeping a diary at any time of your life can give you information and insights about yourself that you might not have the time to recognize until you put pen to paper.

You can let go of those thoughts and feelings that you may not want to share with anyone else. You may wish to use your diary as a place to write down the dreams and aspirations you have for your baby and you may find that the process of writing will also help you to focus on your dreams for the future and on yourself.

conversations and a secret pact that made both of them stronger. All mothers can engage every day with their babies, as often as possible, as my daughter-in-law did. Who knows the effect of shared whispers, positive thought, telling little jokes, enjoying good times together. Every exchange bonds you both closer and closer and tighter and tighter.

Spend some time daydreaming, imagining and thinking about your baby. It helps you to form a relationship with her even before she's born, and you shouldn't feel silly if you find that you spend a couple of hours doing nothing but thinking about your baby and how your life will be once she is there in person to share in it with you. Making that connection with the tiny person growing inside you is the first step towards falling in love with your child.

The daydreams of pregnant mothers are notoriously sexist, with many having an undisguised preference for a girl or a boy. Although it isn't usually a problem if your newborn baby turns out to be the opposite sex from the one you imagined, it can mean readjusting, so try not to get too carried away with your plans!

The magic of massage

There are literally mountains of research that show how beneficial touch is to us. Baby chimps prefer touch to food and touch is one of the first sources of pleasure to a newborn infant, along with sound and smell. For newborn babies, being lovingly held is the greatest spur to development, more so even than breastmilk!

When you massage your bump, your calmed nervous system communicates with your baby's nervous system, soothing it through massage and touch. Your baby's immune system can be influenced and boosted by the amount of touching it gets. The more you touch your baby by massaging your bump, the more antibodies your baby develops to protect it against future infections, improving your baby's resistance to illnesses.

We know from excellent research done at Imperial College London that baby massage greatly strengthens the bond between mother and baby. Mothers with postnatal depression particularly benefit, having less depression and a better relationship with their babies. It's possible, I believe, to extrapolate the benefits of massage that counteract depression, to your baby.

We also know from the Touch Research Institute at the University of Miami that premature babies thrive on massage. Now it seems to me just a small step to understanding how massaging your bump might help your unborn baby. With premature babies massage promotes weight gain, alertness and healthier bones. Massaged premature babies have better circulation, muscle tone, digestion and respiration, less colic, less constipation, even less teething pain. I believe that systematically massaging your bump could confer many of these benefits on your unborn baby, in addition to the close bonding you feel. Continue massaging your newborn baby: research from the University of Warwick says babies who are massaged sleep better, cry less and are more contented. If your partner massaging your bump soothes you, it soothes your baby too and that promotes growth of the frontal lobes of your baby's brain which determine your baby's intellectual capacity. It also tips your baby into a group of children who will be resistant to developing asthma, arthritis, allergies, ulcerative colitis, fatigue and ME.

Baby bump massage tips and techniques

✳ Timing is everything Choose a time when you feel calm and unrushed.

✳ Set the scene Make sure the room is warm (at least 75°F/24°C), with lighting low. Switch the answermachine on and select some peaceful music to listen to while you massage.

✳ Oil up Use natural, organic oils and warm your oiled hands before touching your bump. Avoid almond oil, fragranced essential oils and aromatherapy oils that are not suitable for use during pregnancy.

✳ Be relaxed Don't rush it. Remember to focus on the baby inside your bump. Use soft but firm strokes and speak to your baby in loving tones as you massage.

✳ Interact Stop massaging if your baby kicks and resume your massage when the kicking stops.

✳ Practice makes perfect The more you practise this routine, the more enjoyable it becomes.

Ask your partner to give you a massage

✲ **Supporting your head** Ask your partner to kneel behind you to massage your neck muscles. Gently turn your head, keeping it well supported. Ask him to massage slowly downwards, with the heel of his palm, from your jaw and the base of your skull.

✲ **Relaxing your neck** Ask him to slowly stroke up the back of your neck with both thumbs, making circular movements away from the centre of your neck. Than have him massage all around the base of your skull. Ask him to press his fingers gently against your temples to ease tension.

✲ **Stroking your brow** Ask him to gently massage your forehead and temples with both hands, simultaneously. Using his fingers, he can make light, circular movements from the centre of your forehead outwards then run his fingers out over your hair.

Rest when you can

✲ **A good motto for pregnancy** is never to stand when you can sit, and never to sit when you can lie down.

✲ **A good night's sleep is a top priority** throughout pregnancy. Aim to get eight hours of sleep a night. You may suffer from irritating insomnia because although your metabolism slows down at night your baby's doesn't but keeps hammering away all through the night hours as you try to rest.

Here are some ideas to help promote a good night's sleep:

✳ **A warm (not hot) bath before** going to bed is very relaxing and makes you sleepy and tranquil.

✳ **A hot, milky bedtime drink** helps you drop off as does reading a calming book, listening to music or the radio, or watching television.

"When you **massage your bump,** your calmed nervous system **communicates** with your baby's nervous system, soothing it through touch."

✳ **Deep breathing and relaxation exercises** are excellent treatments for insomnia, so find a bedtime routine that you can rely on.

✳ **Instead of worrying about your lack of sleep,** get up in the middle of the night and do something – perhaps a job that you've been putting off for some time – or go and look at things you are gathering for you baby, touch them, rearrange them and feel happy at the prospect of the forthcoming birth. It's much better than lying in bed worrying that you're not getting enough sleep.

✳ **If you have worries** that stop you sleeping, visualize each one as being written on a piece of paper, then mentally screw it up and throw it away.

Music is good for you both

Ever since a pregnant cellist played her cello all the way through pregnancy and found that her newborn baby would quieten if she played the same pieces, we know that unborn babies hear, love and remember music. Especially if the music you're both listening to makes you feel chilled and content.

That way your baby remembers and relives all those good feelings associated with the music each time she hears it. It's especially calming in those rather chaotic weeks after the birth, when your baby recreates for herself the reassuring feelings the music engendered in the womb.

To provide us with confirmation that music is calming for unborn babies, there's been some very careful research to examine how babies react when they hear music in the womb – and incidentally how they respond to your voice. Noura H. Al-Qahtani from King Faisal University, Saudi Arabia, played music, voice and sham sounds to the babies of mothers nearing term through headphones on the mothers' abdomens. The changes in the babies' heart rates and movements were recorded and analyzed on computer. The babies responded to the music and voice with a quickening of the heartbeat and much greater movements than they did to the sham sounds, indicating a preference for music

"We know that **unborn babies hear, love and remember music**. Especially if the music you're both listening to makes you feel **chilled and content**."

and voice. This shows how effectively you can communicate with your unborn baby any time you want to. If you want to give your baby a real treat you could combine your voice with music and sing to her. We know that unborn babies can pick up the rise and fall and cadences in speech and you can help your baby to tune in by singing rhythmic songs. Nursery rhymes are ideal. You and your partner might like to have a singalong every now and then so that your baby enjoys both your voices and your favourite nursery rhymes. After your baby's born you can take turns to sing the same nursery rhymes to her to quieten and entertain her. She will remember these nursery rhymes from her time in the womb and recreating that experience will help her learn to soothe herself. Gently dancing to your favourite music is also something your baby will appreciate as she will love the rhythmic sway of your body as well as the soothing rush of endorphins she experiences when you do something that gives you pleasure.

Above all, the key to preparing to become parents is to make the commitment to each other that everything to do with your baby will be a team effort. That means team decision-making and shared commitment to the outcomes. Be prepared for the fact that you will both feel overwhelmed by tiredness and that the responsibility of parenthood will sometimes feel daunting and vast. But rest assured that the rewards of being a parent are commensurate with the challenges and nothing will bring you deeper joy than holding your precious baby in your arms and becoming a family.

The best advice I can offer you is to set out on the path to parenthood together, grounded, with realistic expectations, as much information as you can lay your hands on and a good support network to buoy you up when things don't go exactly to plan. You will be equal to the challenges, open to the joys and pleasures and the best parents your baby could wish for.

Your questions answered

Q Can you explain why caffeine is best limited or cut out completely during pregnancy?

Make no bones about it, caffeine is a stimulant. It's the reason we drink a lot of coffee and indeed why some of us are addicted to it, why we're unable to start the day without our caffeine fix. It's also at least half the reason why we drink tea. Tea, particularly green tea, contains a lot of caffeine and gives us a guaranteed lift. Now just think of your unborn baby's unformed brain. We have no real idea what a strong drug like caffeine does to the exceedingly young brain of an unborn baby. Does it seem to you to be a good idea to send an adult stimulant whizzing through her brain circuits? Of course not. Caffeine is just a stimulant to us and even if the baby can happily survive it why would one want to subject such virgin territory to a nasty synthetic rush? It seems to disobey the whole philosophy of protecting the unborn baby from the noxious element of our diets, environment and way of life. Another fact which I'll throw in is that, in large doses, caffeine has been shown to seriously harm the unborn babies of rodents. I'm aware that scientists don't extrapolate the findings of animal data to human beings, and I agree with them. Nonetheless, it's a warning sign and I for one take serious note of it.

Q I am 39 years old and my partner is 35. We are expecting our first baby. Can you explain to me what the risks are for older mums and dads?

Having a baby in your 30s or even in your 40s is not unusual these days, but there are a couple of things to bear in mind that might influence the choices you make during your pregnancy. The risk of having a Down's syndrome baby

does increase with the mother's age and so does the chance of having maternal diabetes and placental problems. But these risks are small and you will be closely monitored and offered advice and screening tests during your pregnancy. There is a higher risk of having a child with autism if the father is older. Talk to your GP if you have concerns.

Q Is it safe for us to continue to make love throughout my pregnancy? I am concerned it may harm my baby.

Unless your doctor or midwife has advised you to the contrary, there is no reason to think that lovemaking will harm your baby in any way. In fact, it is really important to your relationship that your intimacy continues throughout the pregnancy and beyond, provided you're both happy with the idea of having sex. Also, your baby enjoys you having sex. You liberate oxytocin during orgasm and that helps your baby's brain grow healthily. Sometimes you might just enjoy having your partner massage you, or you might like to start by massaging each other. Massage is a perfect way of staying close and intimate with your partner without necessarily having intercourse. Your baby will also love feeling your body being stroked and caressed and will find the gentle movements soothing and reassuring. Avoid making love if there is any sign of bleeding – check the cause of the bleeding out with your doctor first; if you are carrying more than one baby, it is best to avoid having sex in the last trimester; also if you have a condition called placenta praevia, which means that your placenta is lying in the lower part of the uterus; if you have a history of going into labour earlier than around full term or you are showing signs of starting labour early; or if your waters have already broken.

CHAPTER 4

bonding through choices

You'll find that once you and your partner have **adjusted to the idea of being pregnant,** you will have many questions to ask and many choices to make. **The more you understand** about your pregnancy and the birth you would like, **the more informed your choices will be.**

On hearing the news that you're pregnant you'll be avid to find out as much as possible about the next nine months of your life. What will happen to me month by month? How does my body grow month by month? What preparations can I make? What happens at the antenatal clinic? How will I know labour has started? What's giving birth like? What to do about sex? I know my partner is really excited about becoming a father but will we have difficulties during pregnancy that will test our relationship? The questions are endless. It's an exciting adventure but also a bit of a mystery at times.

One of the anxieties that bothers many women is a feeling that you've lost control over yourself and your life as pregnancy gets underway. Your body doesn't seem like your own – it's on automatic pilot. Everything revolves around your baby. Your carers seem to know more about everything than you do. Your partner may not always understand your concerns. So where do you turn?

Friends and relatives who can usually reassure you may fail to do so because every pregnancy is different and their anecdotes may not reflect your experience. No woman should look for comparisons with others. The most reassuring support will come from the midwives, healthcare professionals and doctors who concentrate on tracking your particular pregnancy every step of the way with you.

But by far the most comfort and strength will come from familiarizing yourself with every aspect of pregnancy and finding out where and how you can participate in decisions that affect you and your baby. Your aim should be to have the pregnancy and birth you and your partner want.

If you know your options you can exercise choices and your fear and anxiety will recede. You'll feel empowered for yourself, for your partner and for your baby. You'll feel on top of things. This feeling of being

"Knowledge is power. Mothers who feel a sense of control feel that giving birth is wonderful. Relaxed mothers, free of tension, confident in their bodies, need less pain relief and have shorter labours."

in control again can even make your birth easier, and also less painful and less complicated. A good understanding of what happens during labour and birth, and the knowledge that your body is healthy and powerful enough to give birth to your baby, increase your confidence and your sense of control.

Knowledge is power. Mothers who feel a sense of control during labour feel that giving birth is enjoyable and wonderful. That same sense of control lowers the chance of PND. Relaxed mothers, free of tension, confident in their own body, need less pain relief and have shorter labours.

Your sense of being in control and able to influence what happens to you and your baby will result from your having made decisions for yourself. There are many choices you can make, both during pregnancy – dealt with in this chapter – and for the kind of birth you would like – the next chapter.

A new vocabulary of pregnancy will start to become second nature to you as you navigate your way through each trimester, the choices available to you and the questions you will have. Initially, you may well feel bombarded by a raft of new words, obscure terminology, acronyms and abbreviations but never feel intimidated by this new language and always seek clarification, either from books, websites or your professional carers if you are unsure of anything at all. Your carers will be only too pleased to explain new terminology or procedures to you so that you feel completely comfortable and at ease with your pregnancy and its progress. The more at home you feel, the more empowered and in control you and your partner will be, ready to make the right choices for each of you.

Really getting to know
your unborn baby

There are one or two vivid moments during your pregnancy when you can feel very close to your baby, even intimate. Your strengthening bond feels tangible, real and charged with emotion.

The first is your 12-week scan. The scan provides a picture of your baby using ultrasound waves rather than X-rays. You'll be able to watch the scan being done, pick out your baby's head, arms, legs and even perhaps see his heart beating. You can certainly hear your baby's heart beating if you ask the technician to amplify it. This is an absolutely fantastic experience, especially if shared with your partner. To be aware of, and actually see for the first time this tiny life growing inside you is more thrilling than anything that's so far happened to you, and to your partner. You'll find you bond fiercely to your infant baby and just as strongly to your partner and he to you.

The second moment comes when you first feel movements, though initially you may not be certain what you're feeling. Some women say it feels like wind or butterflies and the first time you may not be able to believe your baby's actually kicking. Of course the first time you feel movements isn't the first time your baby moves. Your baby has been moving his limbs for some time – you might even have seen a little arm waving

"When you feel your baby moving it means that he is strong enough for his movements to be felt through your abdominal wall...That's strong!"

during the 12-week scan. When you feel your baby moving it means that he is big enough and strong enough for his movements to be felt through your abdominal wall, your uterus, and all the fluid in it. That's strong! And as such, it is a reassuring sign that your baby's growing well and becoming more robust with each passing day. You should congratulate yourself and your baby, it's a time for celebration! Hold your partner's hand on your tummy so he too can feel the baby kicking and enjoy the thrill with you.

A third moment comes very soon after this, when you have your second scan, usually between 20 and 22 weeks. An ultrasound scan will show clearly your baby's health, his position in your womb, and whether you're expecting more than one baby. You'll see your baby floating and moving about in the amniotic sac – he may even be sucking his thumb, yawning and blinking.

Seeing your baby on the ultrasound scan screen gets you thinking of him as a real person. At this scan it's nearly always possible for the scan operator to tell if your baby's a girl or a boy. If you want to have that information, ask the scan operator. It may be that hospital policy prevents the operator from telling you the sex of your baby but do ask, if you wish. You can name your baby and start thinking about him in another dimension. Some women find this very bonding and feel they can even have conversations with their little girl or little boy.

Thinking about a name for the tiny creature you see on the scanner screen is something that you may feel prompted to do at this stage. It can be helpful to get hold of a book of baby names to give you inspiration – try to find one that has the meaning and origin of a name too. Share ideas with your partner and jot them down – there's a special place for this at the back of this book on page 178-9.

Getting routine tests
into perspective

Making sure you get good antenatal care is one of the greatest gifts you can give your baby. Try to think of each appointment or test, whether it's your regular check-up, taking your blood pressure or having your urine tested, not only as a check on you and your health but as checking up on your baby too.

You're no longer on your own. You're a unit of two. You're the guardian of your unborn baby and the healthier you are, the healthier your baby is. Each time you see one of your carers you'll get used to the routine checks on your baby's progress: listening to his heart – which beats twice as fast as yours and sounds like a little horse galloping; feeling your tummy to locate the top of your uterus, the fundus – a measure of your baby's size and therefore that he's growing well; then feeling for your baby's head – you can feel it too – to see what position your baby's in, head down or head up, not really relevant till the last month but still reassuring to know at this stage.

Use these routine checks to ask any questions you may have about your health or your baby's, to find out what the next stage of pregnancy will involve in terms of further appointments and tests, and any preparations you should be making, such as visiting your local hospital if that is where you plan to have your baby, or finding out about the other birth options available to you in your area.

"You're the guardian of your unborn baby and the healthier you are, the healthier your baby is."

Why check-ups matter

A simple measurement like your height can point the way to an easy birth. This is because your height is related to the size of your pelvis. If you're average to tall, the birth will probably be plain-sailing but if you're on the short side, the size of your baby's head will be checked and compared to your pelvic outlet to anticipate any possible problems and plan around them.

Urine tests each visit are simple and quick but provide essential and useful hints about your future welfare and that of your baby. Finding protein in a urine specimen will alert your carers to look carefully at your blood pressure, as it can be a very early warning sign of pre-eclampsia, a condition which prevents the placenta from getting enough blood (and therefore food and oxygen) to your baby.

The same alert goes for the appearance of sugar in your urine – an early warning signal that you're possibly developing diabetes.

Your pregnancy notes

No two mothers, even at identical stages of pregnancy, have identical findings at routine health checks. And the spectrum of what is "normal" is very wide.

Your midwife and doctor compute lots of information in coming to a decision that all is well with your health and that of your baby. So amongst a lot of data telling them everything is fine they will be relaxed about the odd finding that doesn't exactly fit. They will investigate further, so ask to be kept up to date with their findings and what they mean.

The first ultrasound
scan at 12 weeks

To the nitty gritty. So that you can think through each test you have and feel comfortable with the reasons for having it, here's a rundown of the major ones you will be offered during your pregnancy.

A routine scan will show if your baby's healthy and that's very reassuring. At different stages of your pregnancy it will reassure you that all's well. Every time you see your baby on the screen you'll bond closer and closer. During a scan your carers will do the following:

✻ check your baby's position and the development of the placenta

✻ monitor your baby's growth rate, particularly when you are uncertain about the date you conceived

✻ confirm whether your baby is ready to be born if he is overdue

✻ verify that your baby is in the head-down position after week 38

✻ monitor your baby throughout any special tests such as amniocentesis (see page 122) or fetoscopy, a technique for looking at the foetus using a thin, illuminated telescope.

Having a scan is painless and usually takes about a quarter of an hour. You'll probably be asked to drink about a pint of water, and not urinate before arriving at the clinic. This may cause some discomfort, but a full bladder will

"Seeing your baby as a real person for the first time on the scanner screen gets you starting to think of him that way too."

provide a clearer picture of your baby on the screen. At the clinic, you may be asked to remove your clothes and put on a hospital robe before lying on a bed beside the scanner. An oil or jelly, which acts a conductor of the soundwaves, is rubbed gently onto your abdomen, and the transducer is passed over this area in different directions. As the image appears on the screen you can just relax, and enjoy your first view of your baby. The operator will explain the image on the screen, identifying, measuring and checking different parts of your baby's body. Ask to hear the sound of your baby's heart beating.

Ultrasound scans can show if you're carrying two babies. Sometimes, however, one may be behind the other and not easily seen. If twins are still suspected at the 12-week scan, despite only one baby being visible on the ultrasound, you'll probably have another scan in 5–6 weeks' time.

Are ultrasound scans safe?

Unlike an X-ray, ultrasound scanning poses no known risk, either to you or to your baby. Questions have been raised about potentially damaging long-term effects of ultrasound, such as hearing impairment caused by the impact of soundwaves.

However, recent research indicates that ultrasound isn't harmful to mother or baby, as the soundwaves are of a very low intensity, and so it's safe for the scan to be performed repeatedly, if your carers decide that you need more regular scans. Keep printouts of your scans in a special place, such as on page 182–3.

What's meant by a "screening" test?

Never before have pregnant women and newborn babies been so well cared for. Everyone involved in obstetrics has an overriding ambition to promote the wellbeing of mothers-to-be and their developing babies. To this end there are what's known as screening tests.

These tests are designed to alert your carers to look further. In and of themselves screening tests don't give definitive answers, they only make suggestions. These suggestions, however, are always followed up and they're pursued in a logical way. If a screening test throws up a question, doctors try to answer it by going to the next stage which involves doing diagnostic tests (see page 122) – tests that are aimed at providing precise answers. A screening test is by definition a blunt instrument. It doesn't give any precise information. It can do no more than pick up a tendency for something to happen. The way doctors express this tendency is in terms of probability.

So if a blood test gives a 1 in 400 probability (chance) of your baby having Down's syndrome, it means that of every 400 babies that are born, one of them would be affected by Down's. By any criteria this is a very small risk, but for pregnant women any risk seems a big risk. However, there would be little cause for concern until the risk rose to say, 1 in 250. The next step would be a precise diagnostic test to detect a specific abnormality. This is normally only done if a screening test is positive.

A screening test could be a special ultrasound like the nuchal scan (for Down's syndrome) or a blood test which all women have like the AFP test (see opposite) for spina bifida. The best known diagnostic test is amniocentesis and it isn't usually done unless a screening test shows the need for it.

So what kind of screening tests will be suggested?

✳ **Nuchal scan** The risk of having a Down's syndrome baby can be assessed around 11–13 weeks using a special ultrasound scan called a nuchal scan ("nuchal" means neck). A shadow of a particular size and shape that's present at the back of the baby's neck may indicate a higher risk of a chromosomal defect such as Down's syndrome, if it's thicker than normal when considered in relation to the age of the mother. Amniocentesis will confirm the diagnosis. Nuchal scans are not routinely offered everywhere.

✳ **Bart's triple test** This test was developed by St Bartholomew's Hospital in London. A sample of the pregnant mother's blood is taken at 16 weeks to measure the levels of three substances – oestriol, human chorionic gonadotropin (hCG), and alpha-fetoprotein (AFP). The results are assessed in relation to your age to predict the chance of your baby having Down's syndrome. If the chances seem high (more than one in 250), amniocentesis will be offered. The Bart's triple test isn't yet offered automatically at all centres, although you can request it.

✳ **AFP test** Alpha-fetoprotein is found in your blood throughout pregnancy. Between 16 and 18 weeks levels are usually low, so if levels are 2–3 times higher than average, it may indicate a neurological problem such as spina bifida or hydrocephalus. These problems are nearly always diagnosed with greater accuracy by ultrasound and the AFP test is used less frequently. An abnormally low level of alpha-fetoprotein may indicate Down's syndrome and amniocentesis would be offered. However, the nuchal scan has superseded AFP testing in many units as a screening test for Down's syndrome.

What kind of diagnostic
tests usually follow?

Bear in mind that diagnostic tests are all about your baby. Each of them will reveal a little bit more about him so see them as looking through a window on your baby, finding out about him and bringing you closer to him. Each test will make your bond tighter. You're in this together.

Diagnostic tests are precise enough to give the answer "yes" or "no", "present" or "absent", "normal" or "abnormal". But they are invasive, and the most widely used, amniocentesis involves a specimen of amniotic fluid containing cells from the baby being drawn out of the uterus – a delicate operation requiring skilled guidance with ultrasound and one that carries a 1–2% risk of miscarriage.

Amniocentesis is the name given to the procedure that withdraws amniotic fluid from the uterus. Amniotic fluid contains cells from the baby's skin and other organs which can be used to diagnose his condition. While it's the commonest diagnostic test, you and your partner should think carefully about it. Find out as much as you can about it and the reasons your doctors think you and your baby should have it. Talk it over frankly so that you feel comfortable with all aspects.

You will probably be offered an amniocentesis if you're over the age of 37, as the risk of chromosomal abnormalities (such as Down's syndrome) increases with age. You may also be offered it after serum screening (Bart's triple test), or if a nuchal scan indicated a risk of Down's syndrome. In addition, amniocentesis can reveal other important information which may be helpful in determining the progress of your pregnancy and the care you need.

What amniocentesis shows

✲ The sex of your baby: skin cells from your baby accumulate in the amniotic fluid. Under the microscope, male cells can be distinguished from female cells and your baby's sex confirmed.

✲ The age of your baby: if the lecithin/sphingomyelin (L/S) ratio in the fluid is measured, the maturity of your baby's lungs can be assessed, which is in itself an indication of your baby's age. However, amniocentesis is rarely used for this purpose nowadays.

✲ The amount of oxygen your baby's getting: gases dissolved in the amniotic fluid can be measured, revealing whether your baby's oxygen supply is good. Your amniotic fluid will also be examined chemically and genetically to make sure every aspect of your baby's growth and development is going well and to answer any questions raised by screening tests.

If you do have amniocentesis it is usually done at 16–18 weeks. Your abdomen will first be numbed with a jab of local anaesthetic. Then, guided by ultrasound, a fine hollow needle is inserted into the amniotic sac through your tummy. About 14 grams (half an ounce) of amniotic fluid is usually withdrawn and this is then spun in a centrifuge to separate the cells shed by the baby from the rest of the liquid. It takes about three weeks for the cells to be cultured and for the results to come through, which is a very stressful period for couples. Many women talk about putting their pregnancies "on hold" during this time, until the results confirm that the baby's unaffected. While I understand completely the self-defence mechanism of putting your baby "on hold" to protect yourself emotionally while you wait for the outcome, I urge you to continue to do the best you can for yourself and your baby by eating well and looking after yourself as you have been doing, and by taking time out to relax and de-stress while you wait out the days for the results to arrive.

Amniocentesis is only done with ultrasound monitoring in order to guide the needle accurately into the amniotic sac, so that neither the placenta nor the baby is harmed. The risk of the procedure inducing a miscarriage in early pregnancy is small – about 1–2%. It's also been suggested that there may be a very small risk (less than 1%) of respiratory difficulties in babies after amniocentesis.

It's even possible to take a look at your baby's blood if, for instance, your doctors suspect your baby may be anaemic or growing a bit slowly. The sample can be taken from the umbilical cord. It's called umbilical vein sampling.

Under ultrasonic control, a hollow needle is passed through the front wall of your tummy and uterus into a blood vessel in the umbilical cord, about a centimetre from where it emerges from the placenta. A small quantity of blood can then be removed for testing and then sometimes further analysis. The risk to the baby appears to be about 1–2%.

The Doppler scan is a special diagnostic scan, only available at a few centres. The Doppler scan looks at the flow of blood in the baby or in the placenta. It's used when a baby is small for dates or seems to not be growing as fast as he should. It uses a slightly different sort of soundwave from a normal ultrasound scan, which bounces off moving red blood cells, and indicates how fast they're moving through the baby's blood vessels.

Screening and diagnostic tests aren't compulsory, they're optional, so I suggest you and your partner request an interview with your obstetrician to discuss his or her position, before you make a final decision to have or not have the tests. This will be a difficult time, so talk it over with each other and don't be afraid to lean on each other for mutual support as you figure out together what is going to be best for your baby.

The best antenatal care
for you and your baby

Consultations, check-ups and tests will happen all the way through your pregnancy to monitor your health and that of your baby. Although most pregnancies proceed normally, these visits and investigations are vital to monitor progress and spot problems early. Choosing the right antental care for you is important.

You have quite a few options for where you choose to go for your antenatal check-ups: you can have antenatal check-ups at your doctor's surgery, at the local health centre, or at the hospital, depending on the care in your area. You'll probably have a "booking-in" appointment at around 12 weeks. In some areas this is done in your home by a community midwife; in other areas, you may be asked to go to your local hospital. You'll be asked a number of questions at your booking in appointment about your health in general, your family history and any previous pregnancies you may have had, the aim being to get an accurate picture of your wellbeing and how your pregnancy has been going so far. You may also be asked questions about smoking, your diet, whether you will breastfeed or bottlefeed. Nothing is set in stone at this early stage but it gives you time to think about your choices and to ask questions of your carers. You'll then be checked

"You're the guardian of your unborn baby... Each time your see your carers, you will be reassured by the routine tests on your baby's progress."

every 4–6 weeks up to about 32 weeks and every 2–3 weeks after that, right up to your estimated date of delivery, then daily should you go overdue.

Most antenatal care is handled in the community and the atmosphere is relaxed. If you have questions, write them down as you think of them and have them at hand at your next appointment. There will be times, however, when you do have to wait around if and when appointments start running late, especially if you're having an ultrasound, or a blood test. Try to make the best of your time at the antenatal clinic by taking along something to read or do, and some food

Do talk openly to your carers

Sometimes it's hard for midwives at hospital-based antenatal clinics to find time to talk to you at length. However, community clinics are more relaxed and you'll be able to find out what alternatives are open to you, discuss your preferences, and be reassured about any worries and fears. If you feel that you're being hurried through, ask your midwife for extra time or a longer appointment to discuss things in more detail.

If you have strong preferences but worry that you won't be able to stand up for yourself, be sure to take along your partner or a friend for moral support. It will help to make a list of points you'd like to discuss and rehearse them beforehand. You may also find it useful to take a pen and notepad with you so you can jot down the answers to your questions. There is often a great deal to take in and it really helps to have something written down to reflect on later.

just in case you have a long wait. It's a good idea for your partner to accompany you at as many of these appointments as possible and you may have an opportunity to make friends with the other expectant parents. If you have other children, you may wish to arrange for them to be looked after so that you and your partner can concentrate your attention on your baby. On the other hand, surgery and hospital waiting rooms are usually very well kitted out with toys and books to amuse children while they wait with you, so you may wish to make a family outing of it all together.

Understanding your notes

At your first antenatal visit you may be given your hospital notes to look after, although some units provide a "cooperation card" first, and give you your complete notes at 28 weeks. Your midwives or doctor will record details here of routine tests and your pregnancy's progress, as well as any special tests.

The details may be difficult for you to understand as many of the medical terms are abbreviated. If your notes don't make sense to you, ask your midwife or doctor to explain them.

Take your notes with you every time you go to the clinic. Ideally carry them at all times, so that if you need medical attention, all the information about your pregnancy will be at hand. In addition, remember to take your notes with you to the hospital when you go into labour.

Your questions answered

Q There are so many tests in pregnancy I sometimes feel a little overwhelmed by them and rather nervous of them. Am I alone in wanting to avoid all tests?

I can understand that to some women pregnancy tests do seem like an invasion of their bodies. But for most women, tests and checks are reassuring and they would want to have all the check-ups necessary to make sure their systems are working at optimum efficiency and they're in the best possible health to carry their baby to term. Secondly, the tests reveal how well your baby is doing. It's like a keyhole view on to his development. Most mothers would want the peace of mind of knowing that her baby is progressing well on all fronts and that everything is continuing as it should.

Most of the tests aren't invasive and cause no discomfort, either to mother or baby. Even an ultrasound scan, which lets you see your unborn baby inside you, only involves a probe being passed over your abdomen. When it comes to more complex tests like amniocentesis a needle is involved and I can understand why some women would shrink from having this done. However the ultimate aim is to make sure you have a healthy thriving baby at the end of nine months and it seems to me both logical and good medicine to examine all aspects of pregnancy that might affect you and your baby.

We know from a lot of research that the key to lowering the rate of infant mortality, stillbirth, premature delivery and underweight babies is good antenatal care. It's the key prerequisite of healthy babies. Why not look at tests in a positive way? See every test as another opportunity to bond with your unborn baby because every test and check-up gives you the chance to get to know him a little better.

Q I've had an amnio and now must wait for the results. I'm fighting a self-preservation instinct to put my pregnancy "on hold" and I sometimes feel as though I have stopped bonding in case I lose my baby. How can I best continue to bond with my baby in such circumstances?

I do sympathise with you. I honestly do think it's quite disgraceful that a woman should have to wait so long for the results of amniocentesis – a test that may show up a risk (albeit a small one) of having a Down's syndrome baby. I think it's the most natural thing in the world, mentally at least, to want to put your pregnancy on hold. One of my daughters-in-law felt exactly the same as you and I had great sympathy for her. It was her first baby and she actually took to her bed and hardly resumed normal life until she had the results of the test. Fortunately everything was fine and she carried on with her pregnancy in good spirits but she needed to retreat from the world while she waited. I think everyone copes with this long delay in their own way. If it had happened to me I think I would have tried to put the test to the back of my mind and live every day as normally as possible. I think that I would've tried to bond with my baby more closely rather than less. In my head I would have been talking to my unborn baby: "We're in this together and we will look after each other. Together we're very strong and together we can deal with whatever happens to us, and in any case, I'm going to love you and you're going to love me." If you think of yourself as a team, you, your partner and your baby, then you can be inspired by the team spirit between you. That will mean you can continue to bond during the time you're waiting for the results.

Getting the best out of
your antenatal care

Antenatal care is the key to healthy mothers, happy pregnancies and thriving babies and its importance can't be over-emphasized. For most women, attending antenatal clinics, whether in the hospital or at a local surgery, is a smooth and happy experience.

By talking to other mothers and to doctors and midwives, you can find out more about pregnancy and birth, which should help to reassure you and make you feel more confident about forthcoming events. Much of your antenatal care is important but routine. At the clinic you can ask questions and explore the different ways to enjoy pregnancy and birth so that you can plan ahead to set things up for kind of birth you and your partner would like.

Use your doctor as a source of information: ask for a list of recommended books to read and pamphlets to send off for. If your own doctor doesn't specialize in obstetrics, he or she may pass you on to another member of the practice, or you may be referred to a neighbouring practice where they offer antenatal care and home birth if this is what you and your partner would like.

The other option is to attend the local hospital or the hospital of your choice depending on your area, in which case you'll be looked after by the medical staff at the hospital and not by your own doctor. The decisions are yours to make.

"At the clinic you can ask questions and explore the different ways to enjoy pregnancy and birth so that you can plan ahead to set things up for the kind of birth you and your partner would like."

Bonding with your carers

Your midwife is your best friend. She's a specialist in providing antenatal care and delivering babies where there are no complications. If all goes well, a midwife you know and have met at your regular antenatal appointments will deliver your baby, whether at home or in hospital. Midwives also work in the community and once you return home after delivery, you may be visited by a midwife every day until around 10 days after the birth of your baby, although this varies from area to area. Many women find their midwife's home visit after the birth is a vital support as so many questions will occur to you as you experience the first few days of life with your new baby.

Your family doctor may be responsible for part of your antenatal care. He or she may attend your delivery at home, although family doctors don't routinely attend home births; if all's well, they're usually happy to leave you in the capable hands of your midwife.

"The professional midwife is a specialist in childbirth, qualified to take responsibility for you before, during and after the birth."

The consultant obstetrician is the hospital doctor who specializes in pregnancy and birth. He or she heads the team of midwives, nurses and other doctors who provide your antenatal care and deliver your baby. The consultant obstetrician is usually only involved in the more complicated pregnancies and will usually only attend a birth where difficulties have been predicted during routine antenatal care or become apparent during delivery.

A special relationship with your midwife

The modern professional midwife is a specialist in childbirth, qualified to take responsibility for you before, during and after the birth. She has specific skills to care for you during labour and delivery, and knows when to call for obstetric advice and assistance. Unlike the obstetrician, her focus is the normal not the abnormal – she is interested in the whole of you, not just your uterus and how it performs. Midwives working outside hospitals are sometimes able to be more flexible than hospital carers.

"Your midwife is your best friend. She's a specialist in antenatal care and delivering babies where there are no complications."

✳ **Domino midwives** Midwives working under the "domino" (DOMiciliary IN and OUT) scheme are community midwives who come to your house when labour starts, and then take you to hospital for the delivery, staying with you until your baby is born; your GP and hospital staff are rarely involved. If all's well with you and your baby and you are keen to get home, you may be discharged from hospital a few hours after your baby is delivered.

✳ **Hospital midwives** work within hospitals and now take the lead in the care of labouring women, although they're nominally subordinate members of teams headed by obstetricians and can call on the advice or assistance of the hospital obstetric team at any time during your labour and delivery. A midwife from the hospital team whom you'll have met during your antenatal care will deliver you with the minimum of obstetric intervention.

✳ **Independent midwives** offer continuous care but you will probably need to pay to hire one. They'll deliver your baby wherever you and your partner choose, whether at home or in hospital or in a birth centre, and undertake to be with you throughout the labour and delivery. Some independent midwives work alone, others as part of independent midwifery practices. Some of these practices also run birth centres.

Because she'll be your primary caregiver, do your best to get to know your midwife. You may like to ask her some questions:

✳ **What training and experience has she had?**

✳ **Does she work alone, or with other midwives?** Will you be able to meet the other members of her back-up team, so you are familiar with them all? Does she work closely with any doctors?

✳ **What antenatal care does she provide?** Are there home visits? What about after birth, when you are at home with your baby?

✳ **What equipment,** drugs, and resuscitation equipment for the baby does she carry? What about pain relief during labour?

✳ **What are her considerations in managing labour?** Under what conditions would she transfer you to hospital?

Bonding with others

In addition to the healthcare professionals you will meet during the course of your pregnancy and birth, there are many more people whose experiences and company you may well wish to seek out as you progress through your pregnancy.

You'll probably choose an antenatal teacher fairly early in your pregnancy and I encourage you to get to know her well. I recommend that you make plans to start antenatal classes in your seventh month or earlier.

The quality and approach of classes can vary – some are tightly structured with little question-and-answer time; others allow plenty of time to practise techniques and role play. Some depend mainly on lectures, others on class participation. The teacher is very often the determining factor in how things are

Yoga for pregnancy

With its emphasis on muscular control of the body, breathing, relaxation, and tranquillity of mind, yoga is an excellent resource and preparation for pregnancy.

Yoga is a philosophy that pervades the whole of life and, though special exercises for pregnancy exist, they're only a small part of the philosophy. Consequently, yoga is not something that you can do casually – to have any benefit it must be practised regularly, preferably before conception. Talk with your local yoga teacher to find out more.

"I believe everyone benefits from antenatal classes. The camaraderie is wonderful and the other members of the group act as extended family..."

run, so do check with other couples you know who have attended classes before you make your final choice. Try to select a teacher whose philosophy of birth fits in with the type of birth you'd like to have. Conflicts and confusion can arise if what you learn in class does not accord with your later experience in hospital or at home. Find out how many couples are taught in each class. Half a dozen couples is ideal as you'll receive plenty of attention from the teacher while being intimate with your fellow participants.

Antenatal teachers are, by their very nature, aware of and sensitive to the needs and problems of pregnancy and will probably be more than happy to talk to you – even if you're not yet attending antenatal classes.

I believe everyone benefits from antenatal classes. I am an enthusiastic advocate of preparing for childbirth, and antenatal classes are tremendously enjoyable. The camaraderie is wonderful and you may find the other members of the group act as your extended family as you exchange anecdotes; certainly they'll make you feel less alone and isolated. It's a great help to be able to share feelings and experiences with people who are in the same position and it helps to relieve tension and anxiety as you open up about your experiences. Strong personal bonds are often formed with others in the class that can be the basis of lasting friendships.

Parentcraft classes are particularly helpful for first-time parents because they're designed to give you information about becoming parents that will make you both feel more confident. Parentcraft classes work in three ways. Firstly, the classes cover the processes of pregnancy and birth, including female anatomy and physiology, and the changes that occur to you and the baby throughout the pregnancy. This is done so you'll have a clearer understanding of what is involved and why things are happening. Your antenatal teachers will also talk to you about the sort of medical procedures that you might expect, and exactly why they will be carried out.

Secondly, they provide instruction in relaxation, breathing and exercise techniques that will help you to control your own labour, reduce pain and give you the confidence that comes with understanding what's happening and why. Bear in mind that bodies, not brains, give birth, so anything that helps you tune into your body is going to be useful. It's a good idea if your partner learns how to give you a massage to help relieve your pain during labour.

Thirdly, your antenatal teachers will talk you through the stages of labour and birth and what to expect at each stage, advise on bottlefeeding and breastfeeding, and will offer practice in bathing and dressing a baby, changing nappies and making up formula milk. This will help you become confident in the practicalities of caring for your newborn baby.

Benefits of antenatal classes

Many studies have shown that taking a childbirth class shortens the length of labour. This is probably because knowing how you are planning to deal with labour pain ensures a more relaxed labour for you and your partner. In one study, the average duration of labour for a group of women who had taken classes was 13.56 hours, compared with the average labour of 18.33 hours in the control group, who had no training.

"Antenatal classes will help your partner learn **how to be an effective birth assistant** by familiarizing him with exactly what happens **at each stage of labour** and at delivery."

In an antenatal class you can show your partner just how central a role he is going to play in your pregnancy, during labour, at the birth and in the years beyond. Antenatal classes will help your partner learn how to be an effective birth assistant by familiarizing him with exactly what happens at each stage of labour and at delivery.

Some courses have father-only sessions where the men can talk freely about any problems or anxieties they may have about the forthcoming event. A concerned father-to-be should find security and support in the teacher, as well as in the company of other fathers-to-be. Antenatal classes give a couple a unique opportunity to work together as a team towards a common goal – the birth of their baby – and very often this teamwork results in a special closeness and an unbreakable bond.

A team effort where you and your partner work together hand in hand, talk openly and frankly about your feelings with each other, learn about and understand the significance of each stage of pregnancy, make choices and take decisions together, is the best possible preparation for parenthood. As a team, you present a united front, ready to take on any new challenge because you are confident in your knowledge and confident in your love for and trust in each other.

Your questions answered

Q There's a history of cystic fibrosis in my family. Would you advise genetic screening before trying to start a family?

I think it would help if you had a little background about the genetics of cystic fibrosis. Cystic fibrosis is what we call a "recessive condition" in which two defective recessive genes come together, one from the mother, one from the father, resulting in a baby with cystic fibrosis. A defective recessive gene is usually masked by a normal dominant one with the recessive gene coming from one parent and the normal one coming from the other. But if both parents carry a defective recessive gene, each of their children has a one in four chance of inheriting both recessive genes or a two in four chance of being a carrier. Thus there are always more carriers than sufferers. Actually one in 20 of the white population carries the cystic fibrosis gene and one in 20,000 white babies is affected by the disease. In non-whites the incidence is about one in 90,000. It's important to seek expert advice if you have a family history of cystic fibrosis. Not everyone will be referred for genetic counselling but it's worth checking with your doctor to see if you should be. The main aim of counselling is to discover how great a risk you run of passing on an inheritable disease to your child. Depending on what you find out, a genetic counsellor will help you to weigh up the risks.

Q My parents and parents-in-law are excited about becoming grandparents. However, I am feeling a little overwhelmed by unwanted advice. How do I draw the line without offending?

Try to see it from their point of view. The first grandchild is a momentous family event and their enthusiasm and interest bode very well for you and your partner

as you embark on family life. Actively engaged grandparents are a vital support for parents and their loving interest is a real spur to the healthy and happy development of your child. Your parents and parents-in-law may well have more time and energy to spend on their grandchildren than they did on their own children, so it's an added bonus for them and for you. Pregnancy can be a time when everyone (sometimes complete strangers) feels they have the right to comment and offer advice. Please don't take this in the wrong spirit. What can perhaps feel like interference or plain noseyness is usually a genuine impulse to wish you well and I'd advise you to try to respond to other peoples' interest in the spirit in which it is intended. However, it's important that you and your partner have a united front where your parents are concerned. If being on the receiving end of too much unwanted advice really starts to get to you, and risks spoiling an otherwise good relationship, then why not just firmly and politely say so? Most people will understand immediately and may well rather regret having pushed you to need to speak up.

Q I have been experiencing morning sickness and it is really starting to affect how I feel about being pregnant. What can I do to minimize morning sickness without risking any harm to my baby?
I really feel for you. Morning sickness can be really debilitating and can, frankly, spoil those early days and weeks of pregnancy if you do suffer badly. You may also find that far from being just morning sickness, you experience feelings of nausea all day. My advice is to try the following: avoid fatty foods, take small amounts of ginger (ginger tea, ginger biscuits), eat bland foods, try acupressure wristbands and eat little and often.

bonding through birthing

And now after nine months comes the main event – the birth – **the biggest bonding session of all.** You and your baby are locked in a partnership, with you **promising to do everything in your power** to help your baby make the transition between living inside you **and living in the outside world.**

Trust your instincts

There are all kinds of ways to prepare yourself for giving birth. Probably the most important is to discover yourself, your body and your instincts and then to have confidence in all of them.

Contrary to what you may think, you "know" how to give birth. You come from a magnificent line of women, all of whom have "known" how to give birth. If you were all alone at the moment of birth you'd more or less do the right thing by following the commands your body was giving you, and you'd get it right. This is the firm basis you're starting from.

From being completely dependent on you for absolutely everything, including oxygen, food and wellbeing, your baby now becomes a newborn infant capable of living in the outside world. Every stage in her development, since the very first moment of conception, has been focussed on shaping a human being capable of independent life. There's no other bonding experience like birth. And if your partner holds your baby soon after she is born, ideally within 30 minutes, he will bond with his baby too. We know that a man who does this usually turns from a husband to a father in a matter of minutes and a 24/7, active, hands-on father at that. Holding his newborn baby close to his skin, his paternal bond will be as strong as your maternal one.

There are several things you can do to really get in touch with this deep strength you possess. On your journey of discovery you'll form stronger and stronger preferences for how you'd like your labour and birth to be. Of course you'll find out as much as you can about what labour and birth will entail and to get the most out of it, I suggest you don't start from a medical point of view but from what you yourself will be comfortable with. So, for example, while you and

"Most important is to discover yourself, your body and your instincts. Have confidence in them."

your partner will learn a huge amount from antenatal and birthing classes about good positions for labour, I suggest that you go over these together, perhaps even role playing, in your own home where you're comfortable and surrounded by familiar, well-loved possessions. This isn't to prepare you necessarily for a home birth but to help you personalize your experience of birth, to make it your own, and to help you anticipate what giving birth will actually be like.

The chances are that your role as the orchestrator of events will be welcomed by your medical carers. Over the past few decades, women have been taking greater control of their health and the medical profession has generally responded enthusiastically to the changing desires and needs of women; the "choices" in childbirth have never been greater, nor our wishes more paramount. Today most of us ask to have our children more naturally, with as little medical intervention as possible, and this option is available to you wherever you choose to have your baby - at home, at a birth centre or in hospital.

I espouse the guiding principles of *Birthing from Within* by Pam England and Robert Horowitz. This marvellous book discusses and illuminates the myriad ways of finding and creating a birthing option which is right for you and your partner. You can explore making birth sculptures, train in pain-relieving techniques to help you through labour and birth, imagine the birth from your baby's point of view and preserve your pregnant shape by making a "belly cast" from plaster bandages. Part of the authors' philosophy embraces the idea that you're free to do and say whatever you need to get you through your labour and birth as safely and happily as possible.

Natural birth

It's reasonable for most women to want natural births: where there's less anxiety because the process of birth and delivery is familiar; there's no unnecessary medical intervention; there's a calm, homely atmosphere where mothers are allowed to do what they please and take up the most comfortable positions; and there is no undue pressure to take pain-relieving drugs.

Female bodies are well designed for giving birth; the soft tissues of the birth passage open so that a baby is gently squeezed out. Breathing and relaxation techniques can make birth even easier to manage, and many natural childbirth philosophies advocate these techniques.

Most approaches to modern childbirth adopt some form of a psychological re-learning so that your pain expectation is reduced and your pain threshold raised. In many cases, breathing techniques are central. All emphasize intense concentration on breathing patterns and the learned ability to relax your body at will. The best way to experience a totally natural birth is in a dedicated birth centre or at home. However, increasingly, general hospitals also offer the use of birthing pools and the opportunity to give birth out of bed and in whatever position you find most comfortable.

Think about having someone in addition to medical and nursing professions to offer support and encouragement. Usually the best assistant is your partner, especially if he's attended antenatal classes with you. However, it doesn't have to be your partner. Your mother, sister, or best friend could also be an excellent choice, particularly if she's had children of her own. Studies have shown that the full emotional and physical support of a trusted person can help reduce a labouring woman's need of pain-relieving drugs.

Whether you're in a birthing pool, in hospital or at home, you're now more likely to be encouraged to have an active birth. An active birth is basically one in which you're not in bed and you don't lie down for delivery – you keep moving – something I heartily endorse. Supported by your partner, you're encouraged to adopt whatever positions feel comfortable for labour and birth.

Crouching during labour means you can aim contractions downwards, using the force of gravity, to help push your baby towards the floor, making labour more efficient. Squatting, kneeling, sitting or standing can all help to reduce pain and ensure greater comfort and an easier, shorter labour. Being free to move around may lower your risk of needing an episiotomy (a surgical cut made just before delivery in the perineum, the muscular area between the vagina and the anus), forceps being applied, or a Caesarean section performed.

Birthing pools

Birthing pools are used primarily as a means of pain relief during labour, not for the birth itself, although this may happen naturally. Lying in warm water can be very relaxing and soothing. Immersion in water renders you virtually weightless and this brings relief between contractions.

Many hospitals now offer or are installing birthing pool facilities. Alternatively, you may be able to hire a pool to use in your own home but you must always be supervised by a qualified attendant. It's worth checking early in pregnancy so that you know it's going to be available when you go into labour.

Home birth

In many European countries healthy women may opt for a home delivery if their pregnancy has been straightforward. In the United Kingdom and the United States it's more difficult. In order to consider a home birth, most doctors would like to see an obstetric history of one normal child, by normal delivery, before agreeing to a home birth for a second baby.

Arranging a home birth can be difficult. You must do your research and be very sure that it's the best option for you. Always keep an open mind about transferring to hospital if things aren't progressing well.

The case for home birth A planned home birth can be one of the safest ways to have your baby. While 94% of all births take place in hospitals, they're no safer, and may be less safe, than home births.

In Australia, a study of 3,400 home births found that there was a lower perinatal mortality rate, and less need for Caesareans, forceps (two spoon-like instruments that are placed on each side of a baby's head to help her down the birth canal during the second stage of labour), and suturing for an episiotomy or a tear, than in women delivering in hospitals. The mothers weren't all "low risk" either. The figures included 15 multiple births, breech deliveries, women who had previous Caesareans, and women who had previous stillbirths. The group as a whole was older than the national average. Less than 10% had to transfer to

"Arranging a home birth can be difficult. You must do your research and be very sure that it's the best option for you. Always keep an open mind..."

All about home birth benefits

✳ **Your partner and family can be an integral part** of the birth and you'll remain in familiar surroundings with no need to travel to another destination while you are in labour.

✳ **Once notified, your midwife or one of her team** will come to your house and stay with you until your baby is delivered.

✳ **Your midwife will encourage you to take your time** during labour so you make progress at your own speed. Your membranes normally will be left to rupture spontaneously.

"At home you don't have to perform according to preconceived medical ideas of what's normal. You create your own labour in your own home."

✳ **She'll help you to seek pain relief** without the aid of drugs. However, your midwife can administer gas and air, or pethidine if it's prescribed by your doctor in advance, so do make sure to plan ahead if this is what you'd like.

✳ **Working alongside** your midwife, your partner will be an integral part of labour and birth.

✳ **After the birth you'll be free** to celebrate as you, a new family, choose.

hospital. The main difference between home and hospital birth is that at home the birth is your responsibility, and you lead the way. The "birthing" room can be properly prepared with your midwife's guidance with necessary supplies available in advance. You're the team captain and everyone else supports you. The major drawback is that if anything does go seriously wrong, medical back-up isn't immediately to hand. Although the chances of this happening are very small, talk in advance with your midwife and ask her advice on how you would get to hospital if you needed to.

There are certain clear advantages to having your baby at home, such as the security of knowing you're in familiar surroundings with all the privacy you require. Your partner can play an integral part in the birth and your other children may also be present. You'll have the major say in your labour, avoiding routine

Having your baby at home

Your baby will benefit from the relaxed atmosphere at home and will have exactly the same care from your midwife as if she'd been born in hospital.

✱ **Your baby's heart rate will be monitored** throughout labour by a foetal stethoscope or a hand-held sonic-aid.

✱ **Your midwife will administer** pain relief in the form of gas and air, or pethidine if your doctor has prescribed this in advance. She is not able to give you an epidural, as this must be given by a trained anaesthetist.

✱ **Your baby will emerge** into the skilled hands of the midwife, or be caught by your birth partner.

medical intervention. At home you don't have to perform according to preconceived medical ideas of what's normal. You create your own labour in your own home and once your baby is born, bonding and breastfeeding usually happen spontaneously. You will have the same midwife throughout and you'll avoid the possibility of cross-infection from medical staff and other mothers and babies. Your partner can be an integral part of the birth – holding, cuddling and looking after the baby while your needs are being attended to, although he can of course do all these things in hospital too.

The birth of your baby will be a private celebration as she's born into the intimate environment of her family and you greet your baby calmly and gently. If you have other children they can get to know this new member of the family immediately and you can have them present at the moment of birth if you wish.

Sounds wonderful? It is.

✳ **Once she is breathing** she'll be given to you immediately after her birth and may start to suckle of her own accord.

✳ **The skin-to-skin contact your baby experiences** as you give her a welcoming cuddle may help her to start breathing and is a wonderful way for you and your partner to start bonding with your newborn baby.

✳ **Your midwife will weigh and examine your baby;** there'll be no hurry to clean her up.

✳ **Her umbilical cord will be clamped and cut** once it has stopped pulsating.

Pain relief

The first obstetrician to realize that the fear of giving birth was a major cause of pain in labour, Britain's Dr. Grantly Dick-Read, brought the principles of natural childbirth to the attention of not only the medical world, but to mothers-to-be as well.

He introduced the education of mothers through antenatal classes and careful teaching, and also emotional support, in the hope of eliminating fear and tension. His teaching is so fundamental that it's now taken for granted by all birth centres, and there's no method of childbirth which doesn't rely on his teaching, either for breathing exercises or breathing control and complete relaxation. Dick-Read's watchword was preparation – not only with information, but also by seeking help, reassurance and sympathy.

An alternative approach, using psychological counselling, was pioneered in Russia and then adopted in France by Dr. Ferdinand Lamaze in the 1950s. Over 90% of women in Russia and 70% of French women are now taught variations of the Lamaze method of childbirth. It has become equally popular in the United States, and still forms the basic teaching of the National Childbirth Trust in Britain.

Establishing an emotional partnership with your baby may help you with the pain and hard work of labour. Use bonding with your partner and unborn baby to ease your pain. Have a dialogue with your baby. Tell her what labour and birth's going to be like – smooth, quick, easy and not too painful. Just practising

"Use bonding with your partner and unborn baby to ease your pain. Tell your baby what labour and birth's going to be like – smooth, quick, easy..."

Attitudes to pain

Lamaze felt that no matter how relaxed a woman was, she almost certainly would experience some pain. When Lamaze read about the conditioned learning of Pavlov's dogs he saw the value of conditioned learning in helping women with the pain of childbirth. Lamaze's conditioned learning for pain-relief has three mainstays:

- **Firstly**, your fear of labour is reduced or eliminated by information, preparation and understanding.
- **Secondly,** you learn how to relax and become aware of your body, and therefore understand and cope better with pain.
- **Thirdly**, you consciously use rhythmic breathing patterns through each contraction in order to distract your mind from the pain.

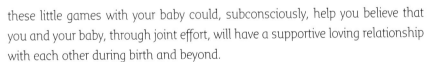

This way birth becomes a very personal experience where you're an active birth-giver not a passive patient of doctors and midwives.

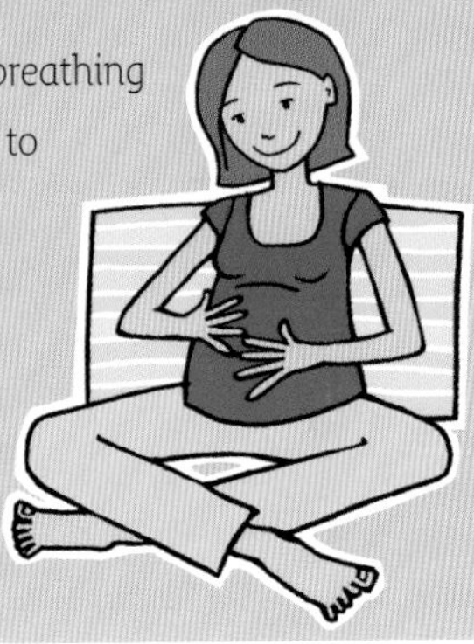

these little games with your baby could, subconsciously, help you believe that you and your baby, through joint effort, will have a supportive loving relationship with each other during birth and beyond.

Through touch you and your partner can work towards alleviating your pain. Most women find stroking comforting during pain. Explain to your partner where you'd like to be touched during a contraction – your lower back, the palm of your hand, your brow. Cooperate with each other so that he can hear your exhalation

DIY pain relief

You can develop your own pain relief with two tools: knowledge and body control through relaxation and breathing. I could add a third – absence of fear and anxiety – but that should evolve from knowledge and self-knowledge.

Whatever methods you use to relax and concentrate on breathing, you have to practise them to master them. By practising I mean repeating the process at least five times a day and I suggest you pick the most difficult situations you can; it's too easy if you're already relaxed. As anyone who's familiar with yoga-breathing knows, it's exhalation which is powerful.

> "Birth becomes a very personal experience when you're an active birth-giver, not a passive patient of doctors, nurses or midwives."

✳ **Induce discomfort yourself** by holding a slightly melted ice cube in your hand for a full minute.

✳ **Then concentrate on your breathing,** especially breathing out.

✳ **You'll soon learn to focus so closely on your breathing** that you'll stop feeling the pain of the ice cube.

✳ **Get your partner to do it too** so that he understands what happens.

✳ **By holding a slightly melted ice cube** during contractions you can go through the same pain-relief drill you've practised.

✳ **Make friends with the pain by getting to know it.** Examine it. How does it start? Where does it start? Where am I feeling it now exactly? Has it moved? Where is its centre? Does the pain change as I breathe in? And breathe out? That's better.

❋ **Concentrate on the centre of the pain** as you breathe out and you may find that you can't actually feel it.

It's difficult during labour not to concentrate on pain, the pain of the last contraction, the gathering strength of the next contraction. However, I think it's motivating and encouraging to think of each contraction as taking you one step closer to meeting your baby. If you can stop pain being your sole focus you can reduce it, even dispel it. The way to achieve this is to stay open to all sensations, everything that's going on around you, what Pam England calls "non-focused awareness". And the rule is observe without judging: you may notice an irritating dripping tap – just note it, don't let it get on your nerves.

Non-focused awareness is for your partner too, who will find it calming. It makes him more aware of his partner's needs and feel more involved in the process of birth. This ability to tune in using non-focused awareness can be especially helpful in the busy environment of the delivery suite where nurses, doctors and midwives will be coming and going, attending to their duties.

and can start to stroke you gently or give you a back massage. Consider using a TENS (Transcutaneous Electrical Nerve Stimulation) machine to help allieviate pain and get familiar with how it operates before you go into labour. The TENS device works by sending out an electric current that blocks pain impulses conducted by nerves and raises the production of natural pain-relieving hormones, endorphins. A battery-powered stimulator is connected to sticky pad electrodes that are placed on either side of your spine. You regulate the electric impulses and therefore control the amount of pain relief that you receive. TENS isn't addictive and does not have any side-effects. Ask your midwife or obstetric physiotherapist if you want to try a TENS machine.

Read up on pain relief

If you choose pain relief without drugs it's important that you master your chosen pain-relief method by reading about it in detail, in books and magazines and on websites, and talking with your healthcare professionals. You should also plan to talk with your birth assistant about the pain relief techniques you have chosen well before you go into labour, so you can make all necessary preparations.

If special equipment is required, make sure it's available at home, if you are planning a home birth, or in your hospital. One method of pain relief on its own may not be enough – you may need a combination for more complete relief. Talk all this through with your carers to make sure you have the best combination for you.

"I think it's motivating and encouraging if you can start to think of each contraction as taking you one step closer to meeting your baby."

Walking around, leaning against your partner or the wall, and rocking your pelvis will probably feel much more comfortable than lying on your back. There are some positions that you'll probably find work better than others, as these will relieve the pressure on your back. Massage is a wonderful way to get reassurance from your partner and relieve discomfort, whether you're lying, standing or squatting. It can help particularly if you have backache in late pregnancy or during labour, as do around 90% of women. Gentle pressure on the lower back during labour can really help relieve discomfort.

Creating images in your mind, visualizing calming scenes, can be a very effective way of reducing fear and pain. As your contraction begins, imagine something that you find particularly soothing, for example warm, bright sunshine in a cloudless sky or clear, warm water lapping on the shore of a deserted beach. The contractions you experience in the first stage of labour are those that start to open the cervix and you may find helpful the image of the bud of your favourite flower opening very slowly, petal by petal. Many women find thinking about waves very comforting, matching the flow of the waves with the ebb and flow of their own contractions.

You can help to diffuse the pain and anxiety of labour by vocalizing in the way you feel most helpful. Sighing, moaning, groaning and grunting are all ways of releasing tension, and you shouldn't be inhibited, or worry about disturbing others. The most important thing is that you find the most effective way for you of dealing with your labour. Many women find that listening to music is very

effective. Have your favourite music to hand during labour. A light, uplifting piece of music that is familiar to you may help you rise above your contraction and focus on your baby. When your contractions start to intensify as labour progresses, more dramatic pieces of music, building up to a crescendo, may help you to cope with them.

One fairly new approach you may like to think about is hypnobirthing where you'll be prepared for birth by a trained hypnotherapist during five or so 30-minute visits throughout your pregnancy. Very careful research has shown that hypnosis is effective in helping you deal with pain, avoiding complications during birth and reducing postnatal depression too.

Hypnosis (or hypnotherapy) is a powerful, natural and safe state of profound relaxation that you allow yourself to enter. You remain in complete control of your body and mind and can choose to come out of hypnosis at any time. A state of hypnosis enables you to be fully present and awake but have a focused point of attention. Everyone experiences a state of hypnosis many times during the day – you drive to work and on arrival you have no recollection of the actual journey, although you drove safely and responsibly. Hypnosis during childbirth is a state of deep and profound relaxation in which you're able to visualize a safe, normal and comfortable birth, giving you a sense of control. In the case of birthing, hypnosis enables the point of focus to be your birthing body. As a labouring mother you're able to have an acute awareness of what's happening in your body so you can become highly intuitive during labour and delivery.

"If you choose pain relief without drugs it's important that you master your chosen method well before you go into labour."

During hypnosis

Body and mind are intrinsically linked. If the mind is able to imagine being in control and having a calm, normal and natural birth, free of fear and tension, imagining becomes what you actually experience. Hypnosis, as practised by Janay Alexander (www.divineintentions.co.uk), can be useful by:

✻ **Helping you to visualize** what labour will be like for you

✻ **Empowering you to trust** in your own body and to have the birth you, your partner and your baby would like

"Hypnosis is a powerful, natural and safe state of profound relaxation that you allow yourself to enter. You remain in control."

✻ **Giving you a sense of control,** by knowing what will happen next

✻ **Eliminating fear** of the unknown and releasing any feelings of anxiety you may have about the birth

✻ **Imagining the birth** going smoothly, easily and naturally, with a wonderful reward – the birth of your baby

✻ **Visualizing you bonding** with your partner and baby and recovering rapidly after the birth

✻ **Rehearsing how** it will feel to breastfeed your baby

Hypnosis is a gentle, effective therapy for lessening the pain of labour and shortening its length. You can opt to hire a hypnotherapist to attend you during labour, or your partner could learn from a qualified hypnotherapist how to hypnotize you. Hypnosis works by suggestion and your practitioner will hypnotize you into believing that you are able to control the pain of your contractions and therefore you can minimize the pain as a result. Hypnotherapy can also reduce the need for obstetric interventions where breech births are concerned and can prevent premature labour. In addition, it can reduce the need for pain relief, specifically pethidine which is known to depress your baby's breathing.

At each visit to a hypnotherapist you'll be guided through visualizing the experience of giving birth, relaxing, not being anxious, feeling secure, trusting your body and your baby and feeling confidence in your own power to go through your labour to deliver a healthy baby. In fact your body doesn't know the difference between imagination and reality. Our need for a sense of control can be met by believing we have a sense of control. With this in mind, it becomes easier to understand why hypnosis is effective in averting complications during birth and lessening postnatal depression – it creates positive mental wellbeing.

Consider acupuncture too but only if this is a method you have tried previously in other circumstances and you've already found that it can relieve pain for other problems. In addition, you must check that your acupuncturist is familiar with how acupuncture works during pregnancy, labour and delivery and is prepared to attend your labour either at home, if you choose a home birth, or in hospital with you. Acupuncture is based on the Chinese belief in the life force, called "chi", which flows through the body. Physical problems occur when the "chi" is blocked but it can be unblocked by firm finger pressure or the insertion of fine needles into key areas of your body which then stimulate your system into producing its own pain relief in the form of endorphins. Many women also find acupuncture extremely helpful during pregnancy and see a practitioner regularly to help alleviate the symptoms of morning sickness, backache, headaches, allergies, indigestion, insomnia and, in some cases, mild depression. Acupuncture for labour may not stop you feeling any pain at all, but it can reduce it, and also helps to stop nausea.

While all these self-taught ways of relieving pain will work and quite likely get you through labour and birth, it doesn't mean you can't opt for pain-relieving drugs any time you want to. However. a complete absence of pain isn't necessarily a good thing, since the pain you feel during labour switches on the powerful hormone oxytocin which propels labour onwards. Feeling a certain amount of pain also encourages your own endorphins to ease it naturally. If labour is very long or you need to have your baby induced, the use of drugs and epidural is compassionate. If you think you're going to opt for an epidural remember that the earlier you have it the more likely you'll end up having a Caesarean, almost 50% more likely. Caesareans are more likely after an epidural when a drop in your blood pressure may distress your baby. Epidurals also weaken your contractions and dilute their efficiency as you will need to lie down. Having said that, if you wish to fall back on drugs for pain relief and you're satisfied the benefits outweigh the downside, embrace them without recrimination. Tell yourself you did your best and no one can do more.

"The pain you feel from contractions during labour switches on oxytocin which propels labour onwards... Feeling a certain amount of pain also encourages your own endorphins to ease it naturally."

Your questions answered

Q I'm expecting twins and am worried that I will not be able to love and care for two babies as much as they need. Can you offer me some advice, please?

I think I can reassure you on several points here. The first is to do with how much you can love your baby. I have to confess that I was similarly worried when I was expecting my second child. I loved my first child so much that I didn't think I had any love left over for my second. The miracle is that love is infinitely expanding. From somewhere love just seems to pour out and the well never runs dry. I compared notes with one of my friends who had six children and she corroborated this. She said "Don't worry, Miriam, the love just comes". And it will for you too.

The second thing I'd like to reassure you about is how much love babies need. Of course they need love but they need no more than you can give as a loving person. And don't forget that your babies have two parents not one. You're not the sole source of love for them, there's your partner too. So I would encourage you to get your partner intimately involved in all aspects of your pregnancy and birth. Then you can both pour love on your babies. And you can change over. When one of them is getting attention from you and the other from your partner, you can switch to the other baby so that your love gets shared around. There's no doubt that twins are hard work. As the grandmother of identical twin girls I've experienced for myself how you're always on call to give love and attention. Nonetheless they do well. And I would suggest that you bring on board loving grandparents, aunts, uncles and cousins, so that your twins receive love from the whole family and so that each twin develops his or her own relationship with other family members.

Q **How will I know if I am really in labour and it's not a false alarm or Braxton Hicks contractions?**

During pregnancy you may well experience Braxton Hicks contractions, when your uterus tightens painlessly, in preparation for true labour. Not all women feel these practice contractions, so if you do start to feel contractions but are not sure whether you are experiencing the start of labour, I suggest you contact your midwife straightaway and go to the labour ward at the hospital.

Q **Does it hurt my baby when the umbilical cord is cut?**

No, it doesn't hurt either you or your baby since there are no nerve endings in the umbilical cord. Cutting the cord is the moment your baby has been working towards since conception and now her system is fully fledged for independent life. Cutting the cord is a straightforward process and if your partner would like to do it, I suggest you let your midwife know in advance. You can request that your baby is placed on your tummy immediately after delivery, to start skin-to-skin bonding as soon as possible. At this point, the cord will still be attached to the placenta, still inside you, at one end, and to your baby at the other. The cord will continue to pulsate for between one and three minutes. Your midwife will then position two clamps in the middle of the umbilical cord – to prevent bleeding from the baby at one end and from the placenta at the other - and cut the cord between the two clamps, or ask your partner to do this, if you have made a special request. The remaining stump will be cleaned and clamped and a small knot of tissue will form. In a few days, the knot of tissue drops off to leave your baby's belly button.

Caesareans

Attitudes to Caesareans are changing. Some mothers-to-be are becoming more accepting of Caesareans and may even expect to have a Caesarean on demand, regardless of medical need. Responsible doctors, however, are hardening against a Caesarean where there's no medical need.

Here's a typical letter from my postbag: "My husband and I recently decided to try for children. But I can't explain to him how terrified I am of what will happen to my body. I do want a baby but I don't know if I can go through the pain of childbirth – and risk ruining my sex life and maybe becoming incontinent like some of my friends have. Will he think I'm being selfish and wimpish because I want a Caesarean?"

As a result of more and more women believing they have the right to a Caesarean simply because they want one, the number of Caesareans performed in the UK is increasing. Not as much as in the US, though, where Caesarean is used by obstetricians as an early intervention to pre-empt legally expensive complications. I'm morally and ethically against Caesareans without a medical need. And of course there are many medical needs, such as breech presentation and twins. But in an otherwise healthy woman and normal pregnancy I'd be against it. Nearly all Caesarean births carry a "significantly higher risk than a vaginal birth", as recent research in Latin America by Dr. Jose Villar, from Oxford's Nuffield department of obstetrics, found. Make no mistake, it is a major operation.

"I'm morally and ethically against Caesareans without a medical need. In a healthy woman with a normal pregnancy, I'd be against it."

Dads, we need you!

Dads come into their own however if mums need a Caesarean. Paternal instincts can be as strong as maternal instincts and really play their part when newborn babies can't have immediate contact with their mum immediately after a Caesarean.

According to findings published in the journal, Birth, fathers have a crucial role in giving their newborn babies a sense of security and of being cared for.

✳ **Babies delivered by Caesarean section** cry less and fall asleep quicker if they're cuddled by their dads immediately after being born.

✳ **Ideally a newborn baby** would be held close by mum and put on her breast to feed. But research suggests dad can do almost as good a job with skin-to-skin contact if this is not possible.

✳ **Babies who had skin-to-skin contact** with dad stopped crying within 15 minutes of birth and were drowsy in 60 minutes – half the time taken by babies left alone in their cots.

Tips for new dads at a Caesarean birth:
✳ Be on hand at the birth
✳ Cuddle your baby within 30 minutes of birth
✳ Take your shirt off so your baby smells those male hormones on your skin.
✳ Talk quietly to your baby and stroke her skin to soothe her.
✳ Try massaging your baby gently – she'll love it.

A modern, managed
hospital birth

Normal pregnancies and uncomplicated births are almost entirely managed by teams of midwives and, although they may be hospital-based, the trend is towards less and less intervention. In a managed birth, however, labour is actively controlled for the safety of both mother and baby.

A highly-controlled birth in hospital is essential for some women who may have complications during pregnancy, labour and birth – an anticipated breech birth, pre-eclampsia or twins, for example. However, in a hospital setting you're more likely to experience some of the modern obstetric procedures. Epidural anaesthesia is available and continuous electronic foetal monitoring may be necessary. Consequently, medical interventions are more common: there are more inductions and Caesareans, and there is more use of forceps. However, most women who opt for a hospital setting feel more secure there because they are confident in receiving appropriate care, especially in the unlikely event of an emergency.

Make a birth plan to you tell all your carers about the kind of labour and birth you want. It's your passport to success and its success rests on you doing quite a lot of homework, by yourself, with your partner and with your carers, particularly those who'll be attending you in labour. Making a plan for your baby's birth will help to ensure you have active involvement in the way she is born and what happens to you as a family during and just after the birth. By carefully considering all your ideas and preferences, and by discussing them with your birth attendants and partner, you will be able to establish a bond of trust and create a happier and more comfortable labour. You have the power and the right

> *"Making a plan for your baby's birth will help to ensure that you have active involvement in the way she is born and what happens to you as a family during and just after the birth."*

to exercise choice over all of them. Get everyone to buy into your plan. Think about the issues that are important to you and then find out as much as you can to see if what you want is feasible, depending on whether you choose to have your baby at home or in hospital. There's no point in making a plan without thinking it through well before the first contractions begin.

Discuss your birth plan with your medical team early in your pregnancy so that you can be referred to a hospital that would be most likely to accord with your wishes, if that choice is available to you in your area. You should also discuss your wishes with your midwife, antenatal teacher and other members of your antenatal team because they'll be able to advise you and inform you about the kinds of experiences other mothers have had and what might suit you best and work well for you and your particular circumstances.

You think... he thinks... think together and your hospital team will be pleased to see how well you've both prepared yourselves for the labour and your full participation will be encouraged. Cooperation is an important feature of the birth plan. By working it out in detail with your partner and all your attendants, you should be able to alleviate any anxieties and feel more in control of your baby's birth. Make sure staff are aware of any alternative scenarios and maintain a friendly relationship with your carers who will want to follow your wishes as far as they can, provided you and your baby aren't at risk.

Things to consider

There are lots of things to think about and look into when you're choosing a hospital birth. Ask yourself these questions before you decide:

✻ **What sort of hospital birth do I want** and what seems best for me and for my baby?

✻ **What birth facilities** are on offer in the hospitals in my area? Am I prepared, or able, to travel for antenatal care? Can antenatal care be provided by my local doctor?

✻ **What sort of reputations** do the hospitals in my area have? Do I want a special care baby unit to be immediately on hand? Have I got as many different opinions, from as many different sources, as I possibly can?

✻ **What are the staff** at the different hospitals actually like? What are their views on labour and birth? Do I agree with them? There may be a difference between a hospital's policies and the way the staff actually approach childbirth, so speak to as many people as you can.

✻ **How long do I want to be in hospital for,** and what sort of rooming-in facilities are on offer after my baby is born?

✻ **I want to be able to feed my baby** whenever my baby needs feeding, so can my baby stay with me all night?

✻ **What are the visiting hours?** Can my partner and children visit me whenever I want?

✻ **On the first night after the birth** I would like my partner to stay with me in hospital. Is this possible?

Questions to ask when you visit the labour ward

Once you have chosen a hospital, find out as much as you can by asking questions. Answers to the following questions will help you decide on most of your preferences. Allow for some flexibility by telling your partner, birth assistant and carers where you're happy with more than one option. All your choices can go into your birth plan so there's little room for misunderstanding.

✽ **Are there special birthing rooms** where my partner or friend can stay with me all the time during birth? Will they ever be asked to leave?

✽ **What sort of facilities does the hospital offer?** Are beanbags, birthing chairs, and stools provided? Would I be able to hire a birthing pool?

✽ **Can I move around freely during labour,** and give birth in any position I choose, with pain relief available at all times?

✽ **Will I be able to have the same carers** throughout labour? Can I bring in my own midwife to attend to me throughout labour? Who should I speak with in order to arrange this?

✽ **What is the hospital policy** on pain relief, electronic monitoring and induction? What if I go overdue?

✽ **What is the hospital policy** on episiotomies, Caesareans and the expulsion of the placenta?

✽ **If I tear or have an episiotomy,** are the midwives allowed to suture me, or will I have to wait for a doctor to attend to me?

Make a note on your birth plan of any special needs, such as diet for example, which may be applicable during your time in hospital. A short list of bullet points is probably easier for all concerned than a long essay on your birth plan preferences, as it's easier to assimilate and understand. Once you have discussed the issues that are important to you, make a copy of the plan for each of your birth partners or carers. This will be important if, during labour, you're attended by someone who doesn't know your wishes. It's important to remember, however, that every woman's experience of birth is different, every birth is different, and no birth plan, however detailed or researched, could possibly manage to predict with total accuracy and accommodate how your labour and birth will progress. While

Forward-planning helps you bond

Look at all the possibilities that will help you to approach your labour with confidence. Packing a bag with everything you'll need for labour and birth is good advance preparation. Pick and choose from the options and don't feel that your labour has either to be totally managed, or totally natural; it can be a blend of many things. Here are some alternatives from which to choose:

- **Hospital birth** or a home birth
- **Starting labour spontaneously** or an induction of labour if required
- **Amniotomy if needed** or spontaneous rupture of membranes
- **Foetus monitored for a short time only** or continuous foetal monitoring

your partner, carers and birth attendants will do everything in their power to make sure your choices and preferences are adhered to wherever possible, you may well need to be flexible and be prepared to deviate from your birth plan as labour unfolds and specific circumstances demand a timely, well-judged response on the part of your carers.

I would urge you to keep an open mind and consider the options calmly and rationally when they are presented to you. After all, your carers have your health and the health of your baby uppermost in their minds at all times and you all want the same outcome – a happy, healthy baby born with the minimum intervention, and a happy, healthy mother.

* **Having nothing to eat or drink (if at high risk of Caesarean)** or eating and drinking as you need to

* **Pain relief such as pethidine or an epidural** or using gas and air, breathing exercises, TENS and/or hypnobirthing techniques

* **Having a catheter only with an epidural** or emptying own bladder

* **Pushing spontaneously** or pushing as commanded

* **Deliberate breath-holding** or no deliberate breath-holding

* **Elective episiotomy** or having an episiotomy only when essential

* **Being able to touch baby's head as it crowns and lift baby out** or leaving delivery to medical staff

* **Use of syntometrine to deliver placenta** or expelling placenta naturally

Your birth plan is your choice

These two examples of a birth plan outline different choices of birth – there are many variations. You can choose to lay your plan out as a list, a letter, or a typed-up document.

I am looking forward to coming into Central Hospital. I would like to record a few points about the birth as the midwives have suggested I should do this. My main points are:

✽ <u>Support person</u> I will be accompanied by my sister, Sarah.

✽ <u>Monitoring</u> I would prefer to be monitored by a sonic–aid or Pinnard stethoscope.

✽ <u>Positions</u> I will probably want to deliver the baby in a semi-upright position, as this is how I had my other two babies.

✽ <u>Pain relief</u> It is likely that I will need gas and air, as I did last time.

✽ <u>Episiotomy</u> I would prefer not to be cut if it can be avoided. I would welcome assistance in order to help prevent it.

✽ <u>Leaving hospital</u> I would like to be able to leave hospital and go home as soon as the midwives and medical staff feel is appropriate.

✽ <u>Visitors</u> I would like my two children to be able to visit me as soon as possible after the birth of my baby.

Thank you for all the information that you have provided in the antenatal classes. I have thought carefully about how I would like my labour and delivery to be.

My partner, John, will be my companion during labour. He has attended antenatal classes with me.

I understand that electronic foetal monitoring is routinely used and I am happy for this to be done.

If I need pain relief I would prefer gas and air and then an epidural, if I feel I need it, with as low an epidural dose as possible so that I still have feeling in my legs and am aware of contractions. I would prefer for it to wear off for the second stage, as I would like to push the baby out myself.

If everything goes well and I do not need pain relief, I would prefer to be able to walk around and to give birth using a birthing stool, which I will provide myself.

If I have to have a Caesarean section I would like my partner, John, to be with me throughout the operation.

I intend to breastfeed on demand and would like my baby to sleep next to me if at all possible. I would also like my partner, John, to be able to stay with us for the first night.

The early days

The arrival of a new baby is a wonderful cataclysm, one that affects every aspect of your life and every waking (and sleeping) hour. To be easy on yourself you should go ahead and accept some of the offers of help. There are good reasons why you should. You'll be very tired after the birth but nonetheless will be called upon to feed your baby as often as every 2–3 hours for perhaps the first couple of weeks.

Recent statistics show a new mum gets only three and a half hours of sleep a night for the first four months. Sleep is hard to come by without help and your recovery is paramount. Practical, hands-on assistance from family, friends and neighbours with food-shopping, cooking, washing, ironing, generally running a household, will also give you the time and space to get used to your new family. It will also help your partner to do the same but in a relaxed, loving and peaceful way avoiding crises, frayed tempers and irritability from lack of sleep or trying to do too much.

In fact, after you've got your help sorted out you might like to think of cutting yourself off from the rest of the world. That way you both can concentrate on welcoming your new baby, getting to know her together and being free to see to each other's needs rather than those of visitors. In fact, you may opt to tell family and friends that you want to be on your own for the first two weeks and ask them to understand that you want to spend that time solely bonding with each other

"You may opt to tell family and friends that you want to be on your own for the first two weeks and ask them to understand that you want to spend that time solely bonding with your baby."

Support networking

Your support can come in many forms. Here are some of them:

✳ **There's the really practical kind** like bringing the two of you a meal so you don't have to strive to keep up your culinary standards.

✳ **A girlfriend could offer** to do your washing or shopping.

✳ **A grandparent could babysit** for you overnight so you can both get a good night's rest.

✳ **If you are able, ask someone to clean your house** regularly so that the inevitable chaos doesn't get to you.

✳ **Almost more important is talk therapy** – with each other and your girlfriends. Swapping stories with the mothers you met in the antenatal clinic is morale-boosting. Chatting to your midwife and health visitor calms you.

✳ **Meeting other new mums and babies** at the mother and baby clinic keeps you grounded. Find out if there's a club near you where mums meet informally to have a chat, compare notes and have a coffee. You'll have so much in common.

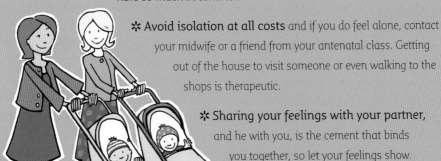

✳ **Avoid isolation at all costs** and if you do feel alone, contact your midwife or a friend from your antenatal class. Getting out of the house to visit someone or even walking to the shops is therapeutic.

✳ **Sharing your feelings with your partner,** and he with you, is the cement that binds you together, so let your feelings show.

and with your baby. This is sometimes called a babymoon – in other words, a baby honeymoon. It gives a real boost to your new life to start it this way, sharing all the care of your new baby with each other. It has the great advantage that dad can be there the whole time to learn hands-on baby care and to get to know his new child intimately, meaning that he'll bond very strongly to his baby.

He'll also see first-hand just how much you're called on to do, understand what's involved in nurturing this new life and help you out as a result. As family life starts to resume a new pattern for all of you, these early days will have imprinted themselves on you and will inform the way you adjust to the new life with your baby, the priorities you adopt and the family routines and rituals you observe.

The sooner you can get your support network working, the better. The early days can be frightening as well as joyful and if you're anything like I was you'll need as much reassurance as you can get that you're doing a good job and are on the right track. Having friends and relatives on tap to give you understanding, sympathy and support will also help you and your partner weather the transition from coupledom to parenthood, which can at times be fraught. The daily home visit from your midwife for the first couple of weeks after your baby is born is a vital support to you all, as she answers your questions, allays your fears, listens to your worries and offers advice borne of experience.

The aim of this book has been to show you how rewarding it can be if you start parenting your baby before she's born. Bonding with your bump is at the heart of it. During pregnancy your baby is a reflection of you – what you eat, how

"The early days can be frightening as well as joyful and if you're anything like I was you'll need as **much reassurance** as you can get."

"Every decision you make in pregnancy affects your baby and that's inescapable. Seen this way, bonding with your unborn baby is an amazing, early insight into what parenting really means."

much you exercise, how you feel and what you do. Every decision you make about yourself in pregnancy affects your baby and that's inescapable. Seen this way, bonding with your unborn baby is an amazing, early insight into what parenting really means. At no time after the birth will you be as close to your baby as you are while she's inside you. In a way, the connection between the two of you is both mystical and magical. Carrying your baby is emotionally satisfying. Breastfeeding, too, connects you miraculously to your baby because it means you're the sole source of nourishment for her.

If you make an effort to bond with your unborn baby you actually do get to know her very intimately, particularly if you speak or sing to her. Massaging your baby or playing games together makes your baby into a real person long before you cuddle her in your arms. Your partner can do all of these things with you and get in touch with his paternal side in readiness for welcoming this newborn baby into his life.

I think it's important to bond with your unborn baby because I know in my heart it will make you into the best parent you can be, and your partner too. You'll be more loving, more understanding, more intuitive and more caring parents to your new baby. The three of you can join in a wonderful virtuous circle of loving care – and why not to be a part of it from the very first moment of conception.

Your questions answered

Q I have heard that breastfeeding might be a good way for me to bond with my baby. Can you explain why?

There are lots of reasons why this is so, some of them just plain human and others to do with chemical reactions that occur in your body. When you breastfeed and hold your baby in the crook of your arm, that in itself gives you a wonderful warm feeling. You can also make eye contact with your baby and observe her reactions. This is bonding too. And then there's the knowledge that every time you breastfeed you are the sole nurturer of your baby's wellbeing and her source of complete nourishment. That empowers you. You'll soon notice that your baby gets excited just at the sight of your breast. Then there are the hormones. The hormones involved in breastfeeding are very powerful indeed. One of them, oxytocin, is literally a love hormone and it makes you feel loving and calm. Your body surges with oxytocin each time you breastfeed or even when you hear your baby cry. Another hormone, prolactin, works in the same way as oxytocin and is actually thought to be responsible for mother love.

Q My partner is unsure as to whether he wants to be with me at the birth of our baby. He's worried about getting in the way at the hospital. How can I best help him understand why it's so important that he's there with me?

I think men are unaware of how much power they have to help make their partner's experience of birth a memorable celebration. Your partner will not be in the way if he listens to your birth attendants in the hospital and responds to any requests they may have. Tell your partner that his presence is the most potent pain relief – women whose partners are present at the birth and are

supportive, compassionate and understanding need fewer pain-relieving drugs. A woman also needs someone to be her coach, manager and cheerleader, telling her confidently that she's doing well and congratulating her on her progress. Most men who've been present at the birth of their children admit to it being the most moving and life-changing event they've ever experienced.

Q My doctor is concerned that my baby might be premature. How will I be able to bond properly with my premature baby if she has to spend the first days or weeks of her life in the Special Care Baby Unit? What can I do to make sure that we bond despite this?

One of the ways to overcome your fears about bonding with your premature baby is to start bonding with her well before she's born. So you can talk to her, sing to her, play games with her, play music to her, touch her by massaging you tummy and generally get to know her. Your baby's brain is working at a great pace even inside the womb. Her memory is quite advanced. She can remember the sound of your voice, the tone of your voice, music you play to her, nursery rhymes you sing to her, and is capable of responding to your gentle commands. So, for instance, tap your tummy lightly and say "Kick, come on kick!" While your baby may not respond to you first time, she will if you practise every day. This is bonding through communication and you can continue it even if your baby's in an incubator. Talk to her all the time so that she hears your voice, and sing and play music. Stroke her using the gloves in the side of the incubator and ask the nursing staff if you can take her out of the incubator to nurse her skin-to-skin whenever possible. Make sure you express your breast milk so that she can be given it by mouth as soon as she's ready.

Baby names

Naming your baby is one of the most wonderful moments of becoming parents. However, it can take time to find exactly the right name, mulling over the possibilities together. You may choose a name that has a special resonance within your family, or you may opt for a name that is significant to you both for other reasons.

Girls' names	What they mean

Boys' names

What they mean

My pregnancy
and birth

By writing down some of your thoughts about your experience of pregnancy and birth, you are creating a lasting record that you and your family will treasure in years to come.

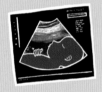

My pregnancy

The day I found out I was pregnant

What we saw on the first scan

How I felt in the first trimester

How I felt in the second trimester

How I felt in the third trimester

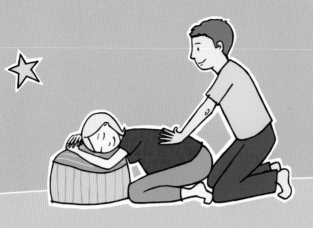

My birth story

How I went into labour

_____

_____

_____

How the first stage went

_____

_____

How my baby was delivered

_____

_____

What we felt when we held our baby for the first time

_____

_____

Scans and photos

Ultrasound scans of your baby during pregnancy are a wonderful keepsake. Make photocopies to preserve them and put them here along with the first pictures of your newborn.

Place your scan here

Place your photo here

Useful addresses

AIMS
Association for Improvements in Maternity Services
www.aims.org.uk.
For help obtaining maternity care

ARC (Antenatal Results and Choices)
www.arc-uk.org
Advice on antenatal tests and results

Association of Postnatal Illness
www.apni.org

BBC Lifestyle
www.bbc.co.uk/parenting/your_kids
Parenting information online

BirthChoiceUK
www.birthchoiceuk.com
Information to help you make birth choices

Birth Works
www.birthworks.co.uk
Birthpool advice and hire

BLISS Baby Life Support System
www.bliss.org
Support for parents of special-care babies

British Acupuncture Council
www.acupuncture.org

Cruse
www.crusebereavementcare.org.uk
Bereavement counselling

Down's Syndrome Association
www.downs-syndrome.org.uk
Helps people with Down's syndrome to live full lives

Eating for Pregnancy Helpline
www.shef.ac.uk/pregnancy_nutrition/nutrition.php

The Empathy Belly Pregnancy Simulator
www.empathybelly.org

Gingerbread
www.gingerbread.org.uk
Local self-help groups for single parents and their children

Hypnobirthing UK
www.hypnobirthing.co.uk
Self-hypnosis and breathing techniques for labour and birth

Home-Start
www.home-start.prg.uk
Support and friendship to parents of the under fives

Independent Midwives Association
www.independentmidwives.org.uk

La Leche League
www.laleche.org.uk
Breastfeeding advice and support

MAMA (Meet-A-Mum Association)
www.mama.org.uk

Maternity Alliance
www.maternityalliance.org.uk
Promotes wellbeing of pregnant women, new parents and babies

The Miscarriage Association
www.miscarriageassociation.org.uk

Mumsnet
www.mumsnet.com
Fun, useful and supportive information for parents

NCT (National Childbirth Trust)
www.nct-online.org

NHS Direct
www.nhsdirect.org.uk
Helpline that offers medical guidance

Parentline Plus
www.parentlineplus.org.uk
Information and support for families

QUIT
www.quit.org.uk
Practical help to stop smoking

Raising Kids
www.raisingkids.co.uk
Support for anyone raising children

Relate
www.relate.org.uk
Couple counselling for those with relationship problems

Royal College of Midwives
www.rcm.org.uk

TAMBA (Twins and Multiple Births Association)
www.tamba.org.uk

Working Families
www.workingfamilies.org.uk

Bibliography and references

Ainsworth, Mary (1979) *Patterns of Attachment: A Psychological Study of the Strange Situation* John Wiley and Sons Inc, UK

Berkman, Marcus (2005) *Fatherhood: The Truth* Vermilion

Van den Boom, Dymphna (1995) "Do first-year intervention effects endure? follow-up during toddlerhood of a sample of Dutch irritable infants" *Child Development*, Vol. 66, No. 6

Braun, Professor Katharina, Leibniz Institute for Neurobiology, Magdeburg, Germany (2003) "Separation-induced receptor changes in the hippocampus and amygdala of Octodon degus: influence of maternal vocalizations" *The Journal of Neuroscience* Vol. 23, No. 12: 5329–36

Brennan, Dr Arthur *Couvade Syndrome: The Pregnant Male* A study carried out at St George's Hospital, London, UK of 282 expectant fathers aged between 19 and 55, whose partners were attending the hospital

Cowan, Carolyn and Philip (2000) *When Partners Become Parents: The Big Life Change for Couples* Lawrence Erlbaum Ass., USA

Empathy Belly Pregnancy Simulator www.empathybelly.org

England, Pam and Horowitz, Robert (1998) *Birthing From Within: An Extra-Ordinary Guide to Childbirth Preparation* Partera Press

Gerhardt, Sue (2004) *Why Love Matters: How Affection Shapes a Baby's Brain* Brunner-Routledge, Taylor & Francis Group, London

Glover, Professor Vivette, Imperial College, London "Children of the 1990s" A study of more than 7,000 mums-to-be

Gopnik, Alison, Meltzoff, Andrew N, and Kuhl, Patricia (2000) *How Babies Think: The Science of Childhood* Weidenfeld & Nicolson, London

Lewis, Thomas; Amini, Fari; and Lannon, Richard (2001) *A General Theory of Love* Vintage, London, UK

Mantle, Fiona (2003) "Can hypnosis reduce postnatal depression?" *British Journal of Midwifery* Volume 11, No. 5

Martindale, S, McNeill, G, Devereux, G, Campbell, D, Russell, G, and Seaton, A (2004) "Antioxidant intake in pregnancy in relation to wheeze and eczema in the first two years of life" *American Journal of Critical Care Medicine* Vol 171, No 2: 121–28

Maushart, Susan *Wifework: What Marriage Really Means for Women* (2003) Bloomsbury, London, UK

McCarthy, P (1998) "Hypnosis in obstetrics" *Australian Journal of Clinical and Experimental Hypnosis* Vol 26, 35–42

Mehl-Madrona, Lewis E (2004) "Hypnosis to facilitate uncomplicated birth" **American Journal of Clinical Hypnosis** April issue

Meltzoff, Andrew, Professor of Psychology at Washington University
"Development of imitation and the understanding of persons" A current
research project begun in 1998

Nielsen, Tore, PhD, Dream and Nightmare Laboratory, Canada (2007)
"Dream-associated behaviors affecting pregnant and postpartum women"
Sleep Vol 30, No 9: 1162–69.

Seaton Study "Eating apples and fish during pregnancy may protect against
childhood asthma and allergies" A study carried out at the University of
Aberdeen, UK and presented at the *American Thoracic Society International
Conference* May 2007

Survey of 2,100 dads "Men in the Media Today" An Australian study

Taylor, Professor Laurie (2003) *What Are Children For?* Short Books,
London, UK

Touch Research Institute, University of Miami
School of Medicine, P.O. Box 016820, Miami Fl, 33101

Torr, James (2003) *Is There a Father in the House?*
Radcliffe Publishing Ltd, UK

Wallerstein, Judith; Lewis, Julia; and Blakesee, Sandra (2000)
Unexpected Legacy of Divorce: A 25 Year Landmark Study Hyperion, USA

Index

Acknowledgments

My long-time friend and editor, Corinne Roberts, has given me meticulous help with well-judged counsel and my book is the better for it. My thanks to Janice Day for typing up the manuscript. Marianne Markham as always came up with great designs. Miriam Farbey and Peggy Vance have steered the whole project with compassion and professionalism. I thank them all.

The publisher would like to thank Andi Sisodia for proofreading, Sue Bosanko for the index, and the following for their kind permission to reproduce their photographs: (Key: a-above; b-below/bottom; c-centre; l-left; r-right; t-top) Alamy Images: WoodyStock 8; Corbis: Wolfgang Flamisch/zefa 110; Owen Franken 2, 140; PunchStock: PhotoAlto 42; Science Photo Library: Ian Hooton 78